SURREALISM

Author: Natalia Brodskaya

Layout:
Baseline Co. Ltd,
District 3, Ho Chi Minh City
Vietnam

ISBN: 978-1-68325-938-1

Printed in

Natalia Brodskaya

SURREALISM

Dreams, symbols, and the liberation of the unconscious

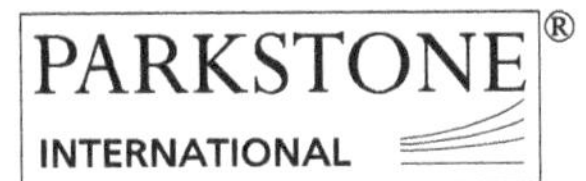

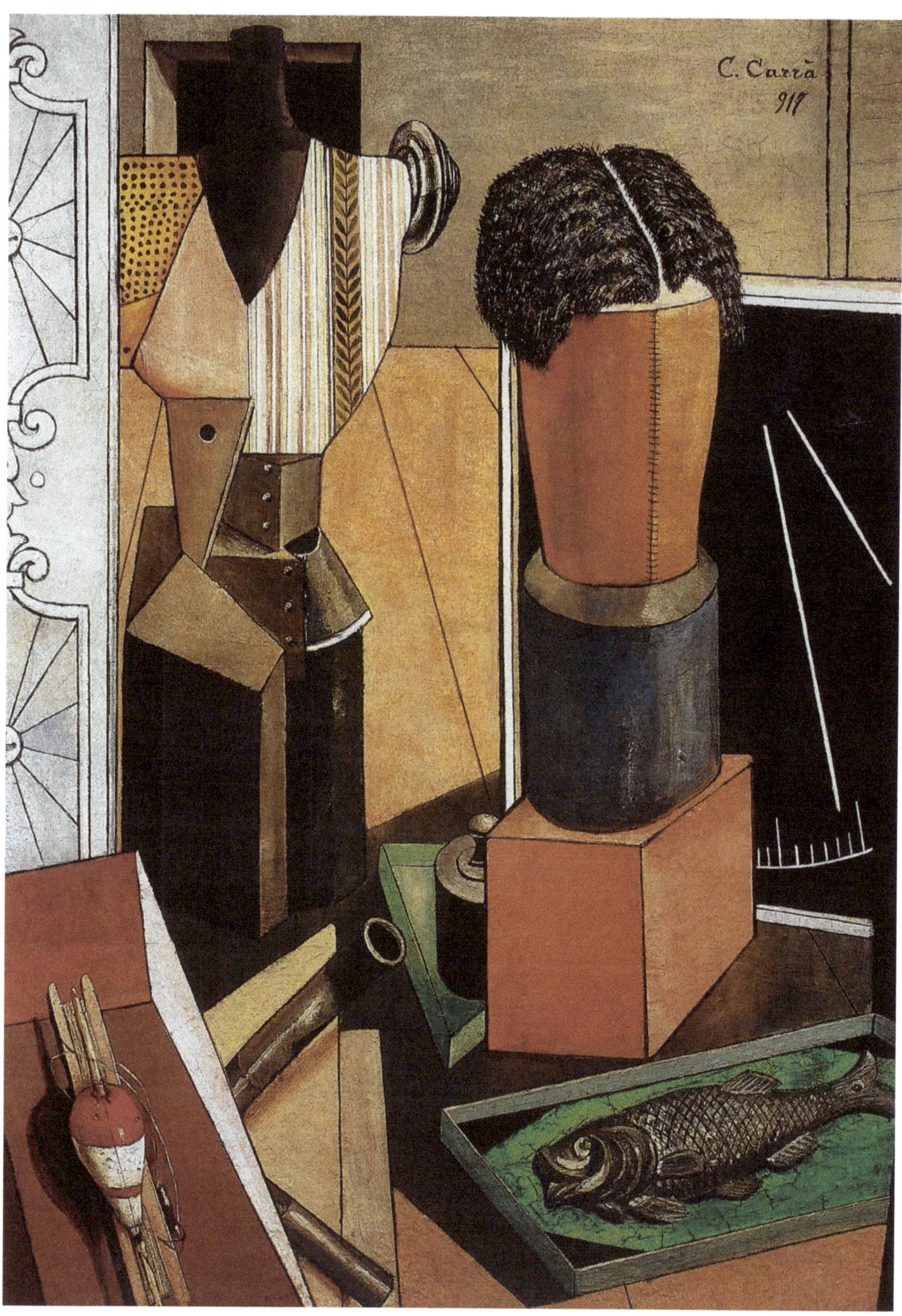

C. Carrà
917

CONTENTS

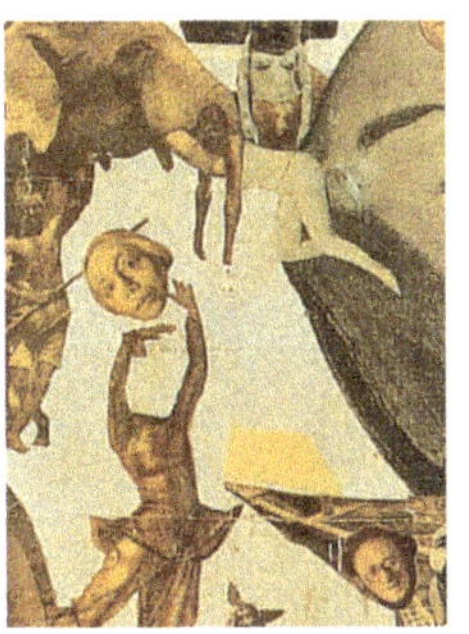
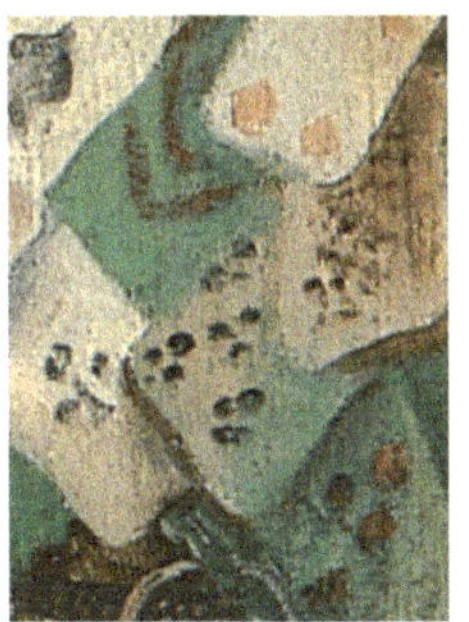
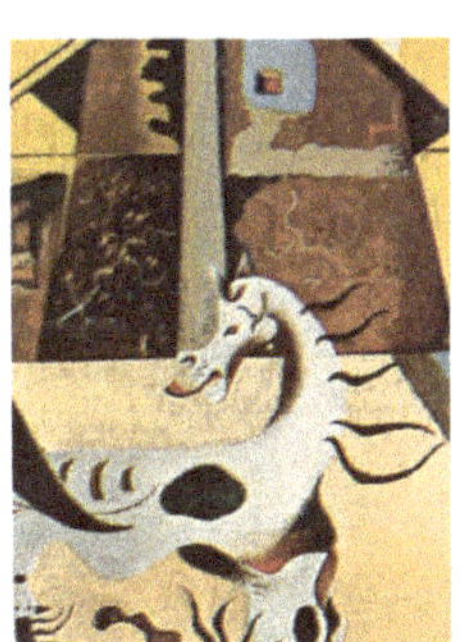
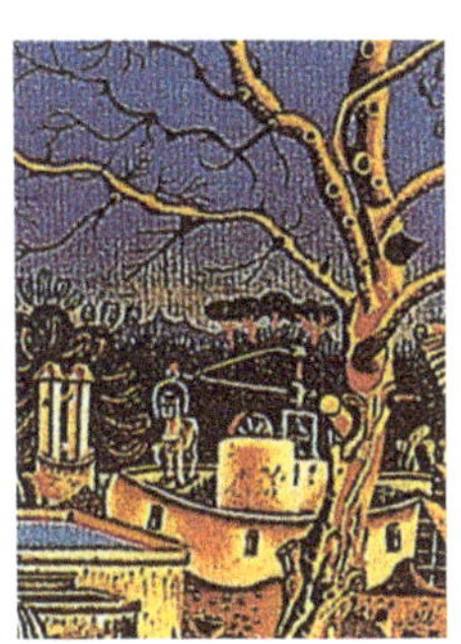
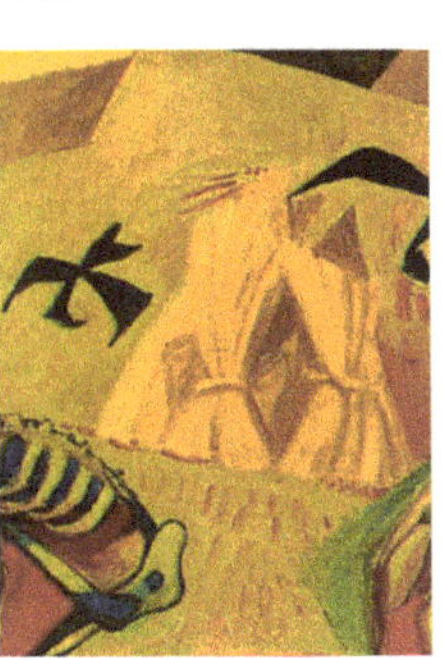

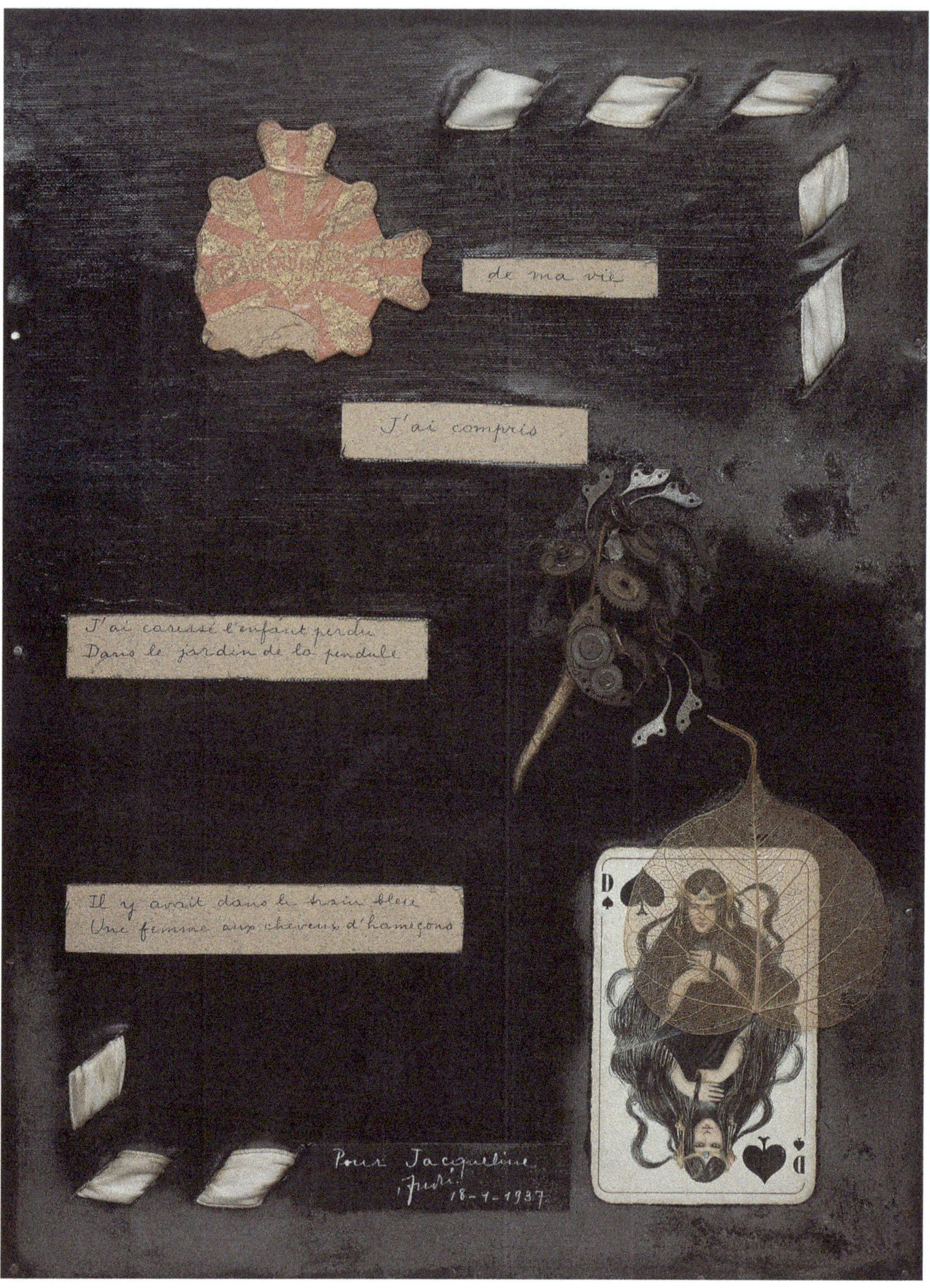

de ma vie

J'ai compris

J'ai caressé l'enfant perdu
Dans le jardin de la pendule

Il y avait dans le train bleu
Une femme aux cheveux d'hameçons

Pour Jacqueline
jeudi 18-1-1937

I. SURREALISM - ORIGINS AND SOURCES

Surrealism found its name almost as spontaneously as had Dada, the only difference being that unlike "Dada", the term "Surrealism" possessed an exact meaning. The word "Surrealism" means "above realism", "higher than realism". The inventor of the term was Guillaume Apollinaire. He said that he was aiming to be above the blind replication of nature; he did not want to imitate nature in the manner of photographers. In his search for a term, he strove to be as exact as possible.

Apollinaire's term was of sufficiently wide scope to be able to accommodate the ambition of many generations of creative artists who with their artworks were going outside the framework of the visible, real world. Before Apollinaire passed away on 9 November 1918, he had sketched out the contours of the Surrealist movement that was about to come into existence, and had given it a name.

But it was not until 1924 that André Breton linked the term Surrealism to the new direction being taken by literature and the fine arts. He thought that for the new artistic language, "supernaturalism", the term that was employed by Gérard de Nerval, was possibly more suitable. Nerval intended this term to cover not only his own art, but creative work of any kind that was made subject not to the copying of reality, but to the imagination, the same approach Apollinaire had in mind.

▲ **Carlo Carrà**,
The Enchanted Room, 1917.
Oil on canvas, 65 x 52 cm.
Private Collection, Milan.

◀ **André Breton**,
Untitled (Poem Object, for Jacqueline), 1937.
Collage, cloth on cardboard, with ribbon, sheet, tarot card,
metal mecanism, punched cardboard, ink, place in a box
(not represented here), 39.5 x 30.5 cm.
The Art Institute of Chicago, Chicago.

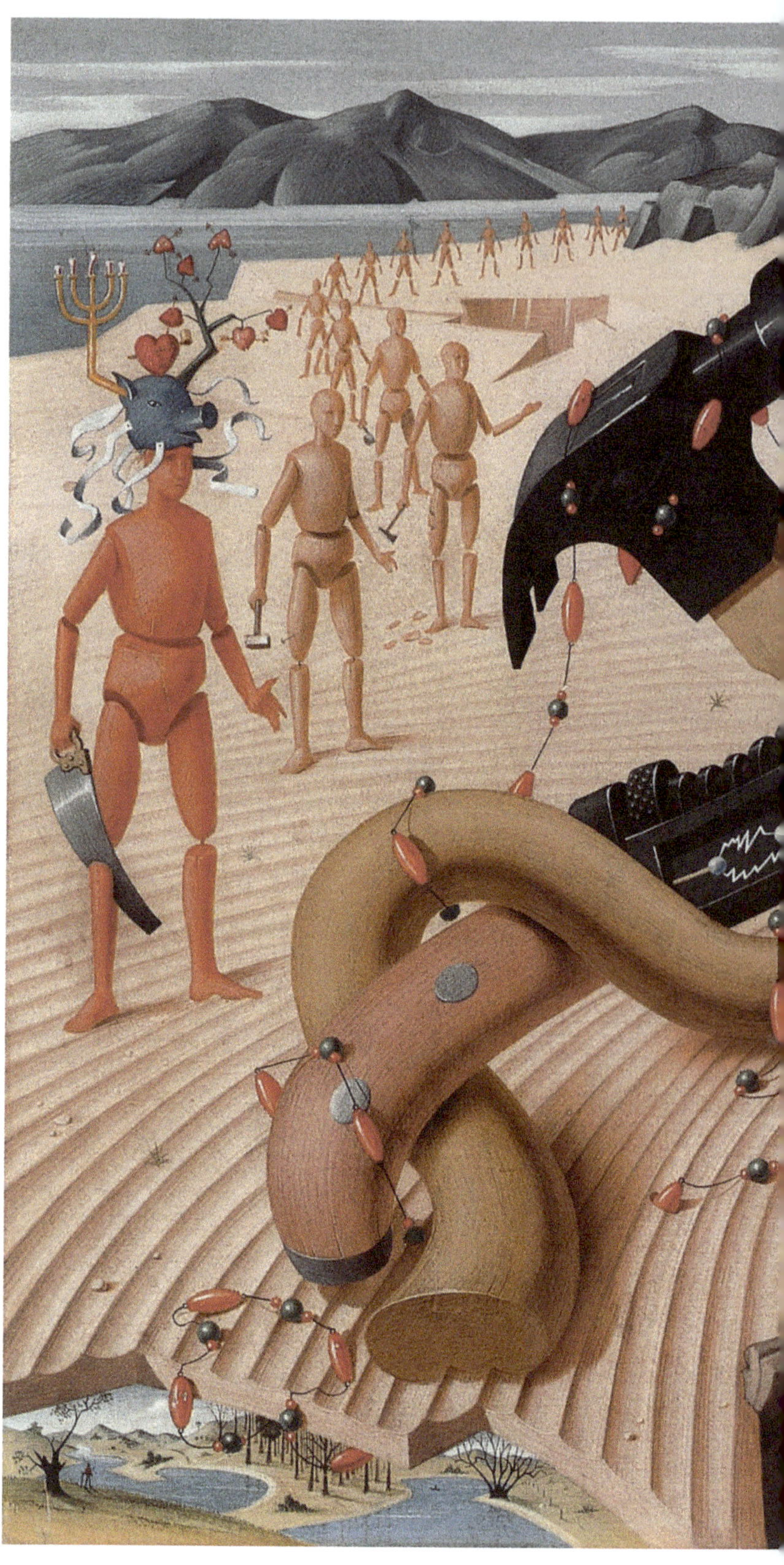

George Marinko, ▶
Sentimental Aspects of Misfortune, c. 1937.
Tempera on masonite, 35.7 x 40.3 cm.
Wadsworth Atheneum Museum of Art,
Hartford.

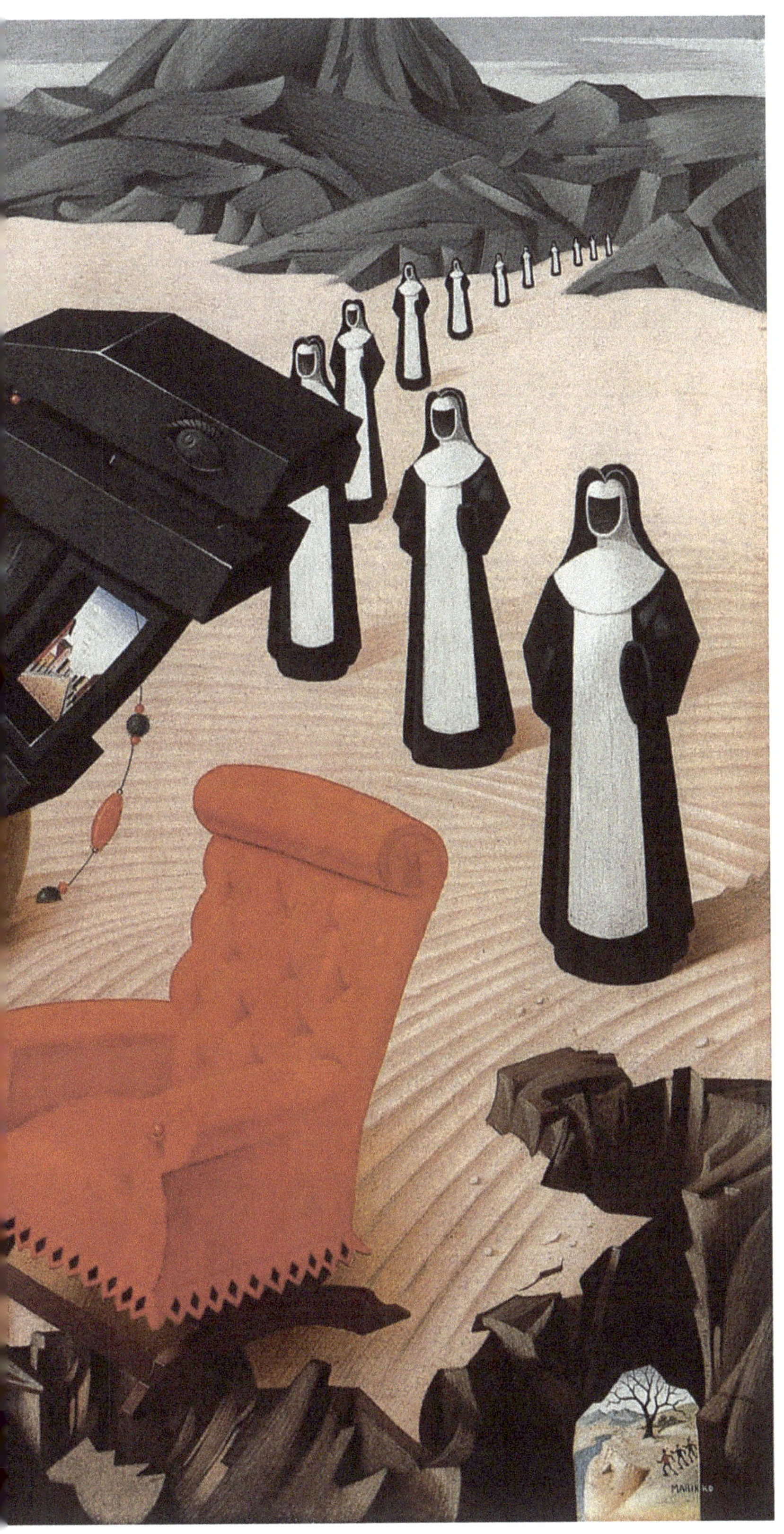

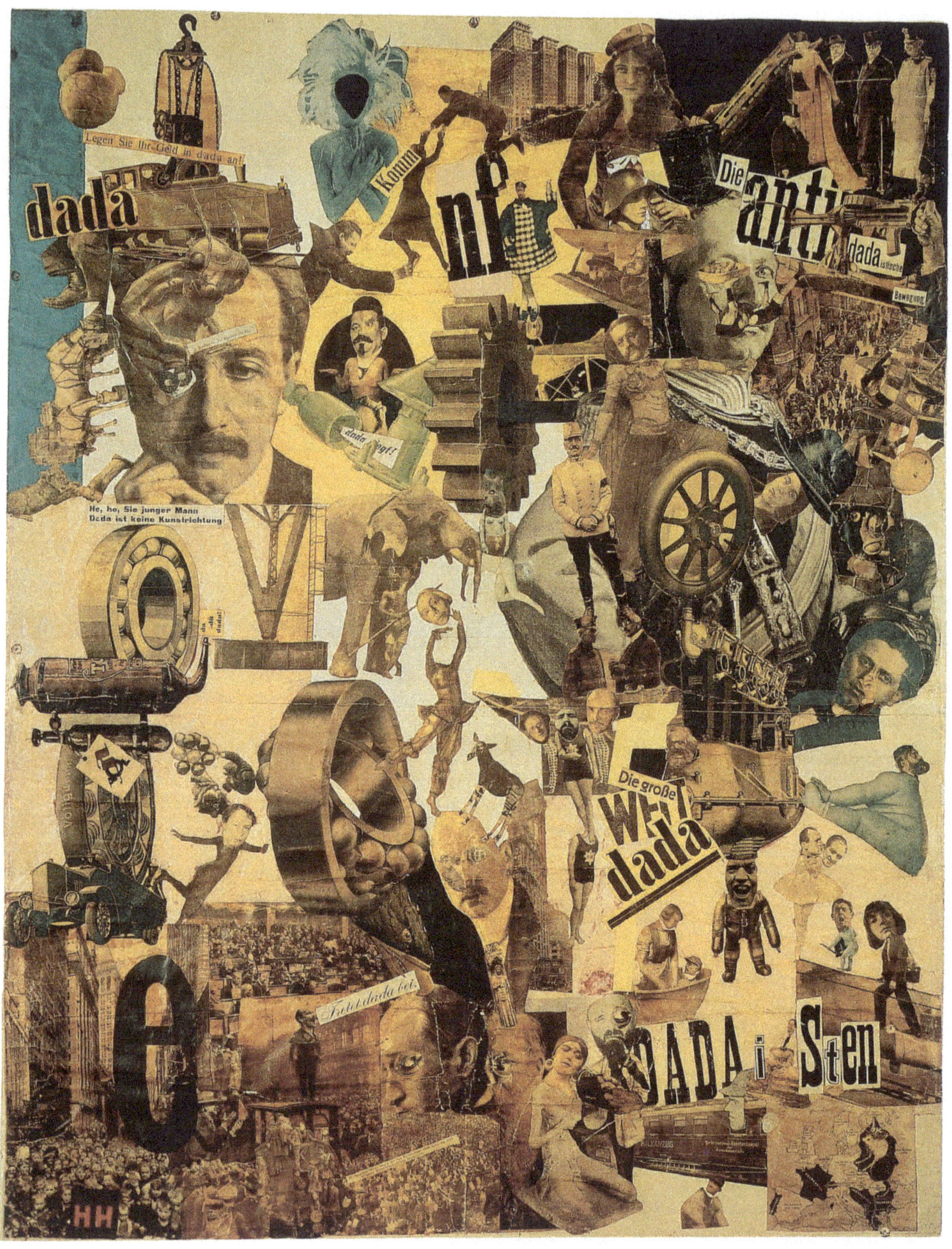

Legen Sie Ihr Geld in dada an!
dada
Komm
nf
Die anti
dada ist keine
Bewegung
dada siegt!
He, he, Sie junger Mann
Dada ist keine Kunstrichtung
Die große
Welt
dada
Tretet dada bei
DADA i Sten
HH

II. THE DEVELOPMENT OF SURREALISM

Over the course of 1922 and 1923, the journal of the movement that was taking shape was *Littérature*, a collaboration between Breton, Aragon, Éluard, Picabia, Peret, and Ernst, together with Robert Desnos, who wrote under the pseudonym of Rose Sélavy which he had taken from Marcel Duchamp. New, youthful forces were constantly finding their way into the journal. Surrealism manifested itself most obviously in literature in the initial phase of its development. Its head, without a doubt, was André Breton.

He wore green spectacles purely to catch attention. The André Breton of the 1920s possessed qualities which made everyone who had joined the new world of Surrealism drawn to him, and led them to gather around him. His contemporaries spoke of the peculiar magnetism of his personality. He was a man who proved capable of persuading others,

and of forming a circle of supporters who made up the driving force of the movement.

A man's whole experience of real, everyday life enters into contradiction with his imaginative capability, with the experience of a different life, the life of his dreams.

Breton therefore rejected everything in art that was connected to realism and, in the final analysis, to all the classics that the Dadaists were trying so hard to destroy. For genuine creative work one requires freedom, and it is essential to throw off the weight of everything that oppresses man in real life, everything upon which the structure of realism is founded.

The Surrealist poet, in his research for sources of imagination, turned to the experience of Freud, who was the first man to appreciate the vast place in the life of man occupied by dreams. The objective of Surrealism is to make use of the dream, which will open the way to the Great Mystery of Life in the cause of his own art.

In this fashion, Breton consolidated the language of Surrealism, for the sake of which the Dadaists

◀ **Hannah Höch,**
Cut with the Kitchen Knife – Dada Through the Last Weimar Beer Belly Cultural Epoch of Germany, 1919-1920.
Photomontage, 114 x 90.2 cm.
Staaliche Museen zu Berlin, Preussischer Kulturbesitz, Nationalgalerie, Berlin.

had been striving to destroy the outdated language of art. Breton's automatism of composition was basically a literary affair. When it came to the language of other fields of art, such as painting and sculpture, Breton's disciples would have to find it by themselves in their own individual fields. From 1 December 1924, the journal *La Révolution surréaliste*, run by Pierre Naville and Benjamin Peret, and printing the work of Aragon, Éluard, Soupault, Vitrac, and numerous others, became the printed mouthpiece of the Surrealists.

Every Surrealists' get-together, at the apartment of one of the groups, or at one of their favourite cafes was usually accompanied by games. In 1925, the Surrealists published their first "exquisite corpses" – the result of their favourite game. For the Surrealists, this game was an example, first of all, of automatic, absolutely unpremeditated creativity, and second, of the creativity of a team.

In 1925, there also occurred an event of exceptional importance: the first joint exhibition of Surrealist painting was held in Paris at the Galerie Pierre. The artists involved were Arp, de Chirico, Ernst, Klee, Man Ray, Miró, Picasso, and Pierre Roy. It was the beginning of the succession of displays of painting and sculpture that make it possible to speak of Surrealism both as a phenomenon and at the same time as the union of diverse and outstanding aesthetic talents.

On 26 March 1926, the Galerie Surréaliste was solemnly opened, and it showed works by Duchamp and Picabia, as well as those artists already named. In 1928, the Galerie Bernheim put on an individual exhibition of Max Ernst. The ranks of the Surrealist artists in Paris were reinforced by incomers from other countries. In 1927, René Magritte arrived from Belgium. In 1928, Salvador Dalí came from Spain to Paris for the first time, and he had his first personal exhibition in Paris in 1929. In 1931, Alberto Giacometti, a native of Switzerland, exhibited his Surrealist sculpture-objects for the first time. The Surrealist artists illustrated books, painted scenery for contemporary theatrical productions, and made Surrealist films.

However, Surrealism as a movement had already experienced the moment of its triumph. Even in the early stages, absolute unity had not been one of its characteristics, but now disagreements were becoming increasingly acute. The events in the political and social life of Europe at the beginning of the 20th century were bound to be reflected in a movement which took such an uncompromising, even anarchist position on the subject of the bourgeois world. First the Revolution in Russia and the wave of unrest that hit the whole of Europe as a result, along with Lenin and Trotsky's writing; then the war in Morocco, and the necessity for the French intelligentsia to determine their own position in relation to it. All this provoked not only heated polemics from the Surrealists that were directed against other groups of intellectuals in Paris, but also sharp disagreements within the movement.

Giorgio de Chirico, ▶
Premonitory Portrait of Guillaume Apollinaire, 1914.
Oil and charcoal on canvas, 81.5 x 65 cm.
Centre Georges-Pompidou,
Musée national d'art moderne, Paris.

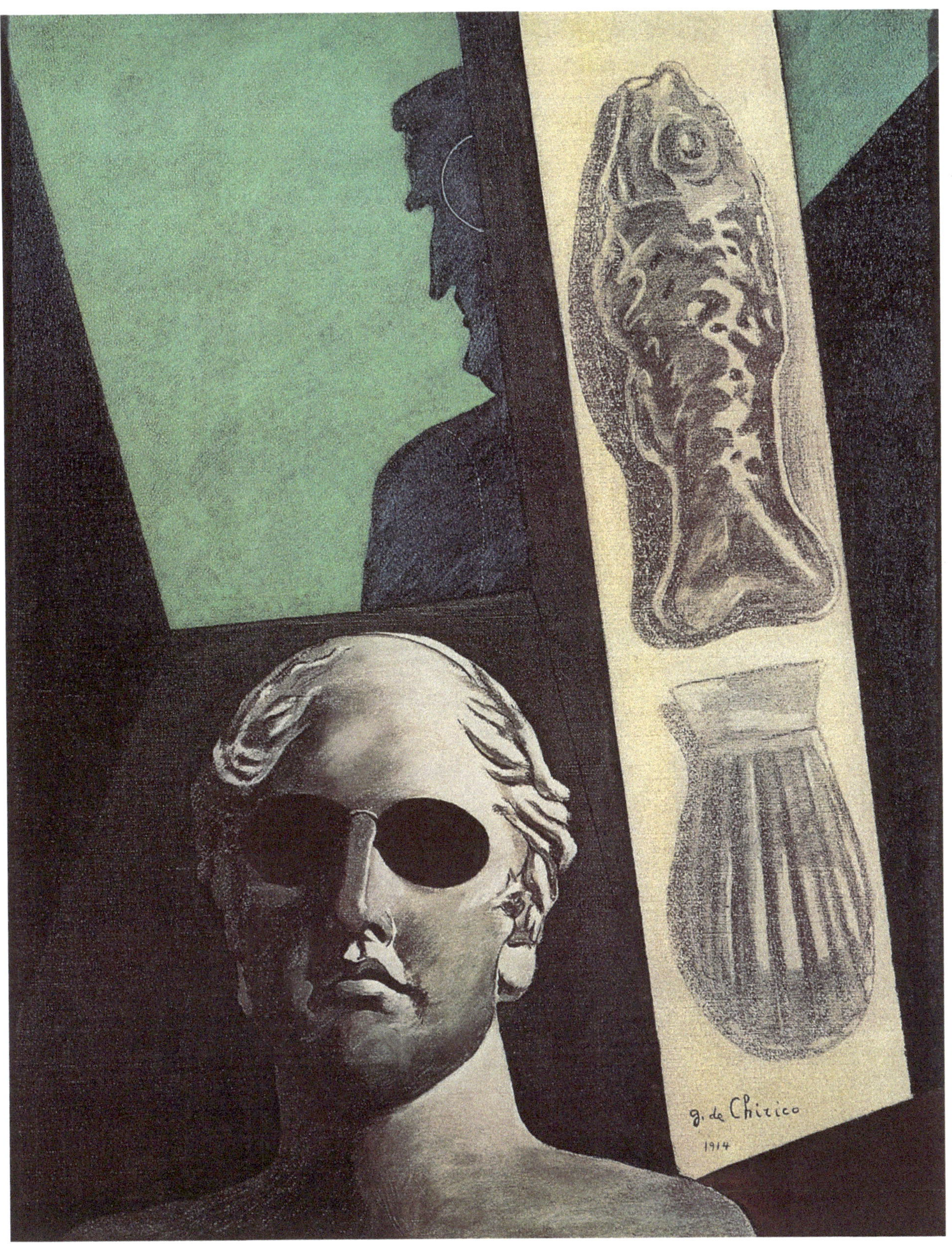

g. de Chirico
1914

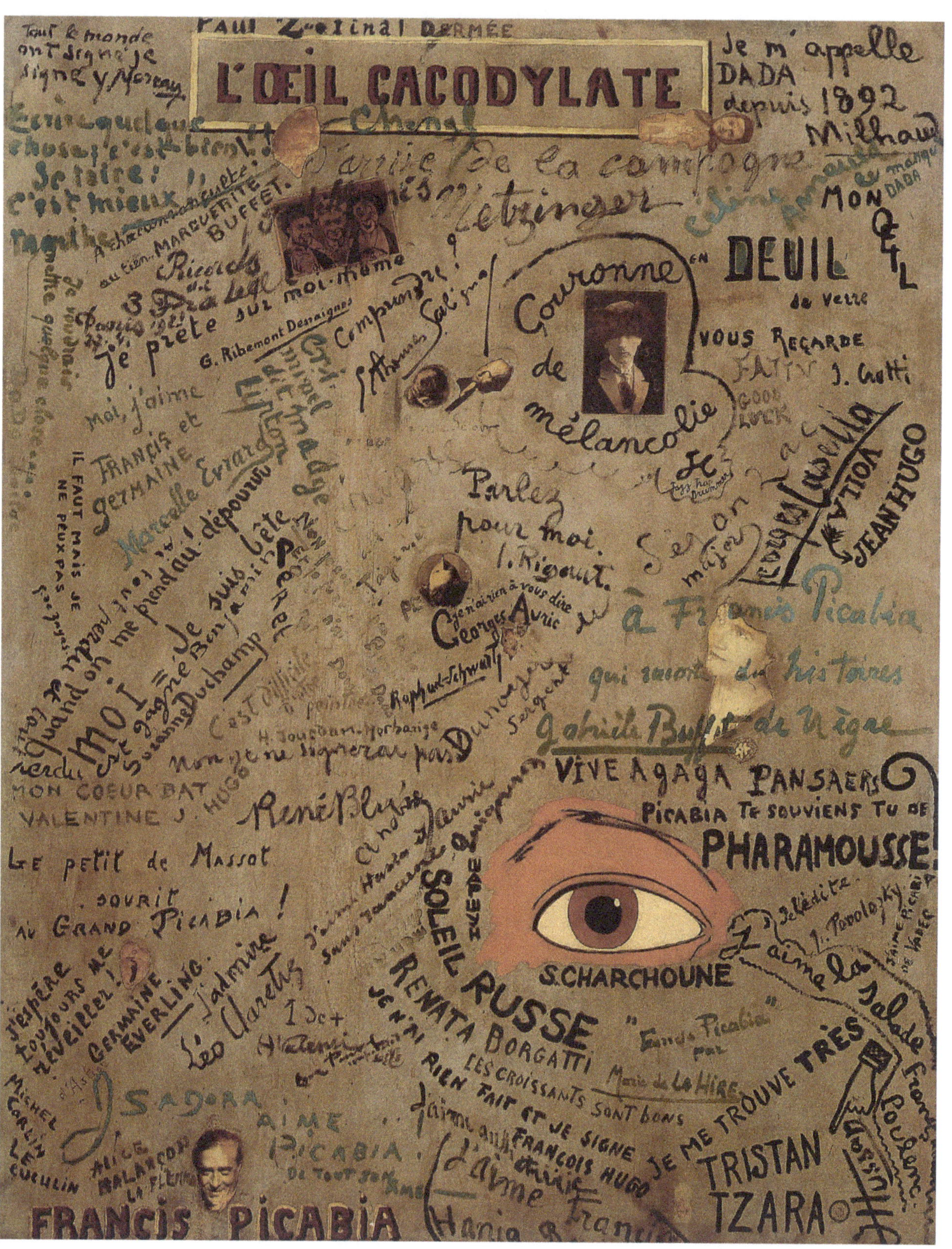
PAUL Z-ecInal DERMÉE
L'ŒIL CACODYLATE
Tout le monde
ont signé je
signe Y. Moreau
Enregistrer quelque
chose c'est bien !!
Se taire :
c'est mieux
Je m'appelle
DADA
depuis 1892
Milhaud
MON ŒIL
Achevonnaisette MARGUERITTE
au tén. BUFFET.
Picons
moi, j'aime
FRANCIS et
germaine
Marcelle Erard
J'arrive de la campagne
Metzinger
MON DADA
DEUIL
du verre
VOUS REGARDE
FATTY J. Gotti
GOOD LUCK
Couronne EN
de
mélancolie
VOILÀ
JEAN HUGO
Parlez
pour moi.
J. Rigaut.
Georges Auric
à Francis Picabia
qui raconte des histoires
Gabrielle Buffet de nègre
MOI Je suis bête
Suzanne Duchamp
C'est officiel
Non je ne signerai pas D. Duchamp
H. Jourdain-Morbange
MON CŒUR BAT
VALENTINE J. HUGO
René Blya
Le petit de Massot
sourit
au GRAND PICABIA !
J'espère me
toujours me
réveiller
Germaine
EVERLING.
J'admire
Léo Claretie
J. SADORA
AIME
PICABIA
DE TOUT SON
ÂME
VIVE A g A g A PANSAERS
PICABIA Te souviens tu de
PHARAMOUSSE
S. CHARCHOUNE
SOLEIL RUSSE
RENATA BORGATTI
LES CROISSANTS SONT bons
"Fonds Picabia"
par
Marie de La HIRE
Je me trouve TRÈS
J. Povolozky
J'aime la
salade
Poulenc
FRANÇOIS HUGO
J'aime
Michel
Corlin
Le
Cuculin
ALICE
BALANCOU
LA FLEUR
FRANCIS PICABIA
Hania
TRISTAN
TZARA

Breton affirmed his solidarity with the Communist Party. The most decisive position on the political level was taken by the Five ("Les Cinq"): Aragon, Breton, Éluard, Peret, and Unik. In November 1926, they excluded Antonin Artaud and Philippe Soupault from the Surrealist movement for "incompatibility of aims". They thought that it was now no longer enough to state one's position: one had to take the side of the party of revolution. The framework of Surrealism seemed to some of them to be too narrow. Desnos and Naville left the movement. Breton was implacable towards his former friends. He demanded that the performance which Artaud was arranging should be taken off the stage, despite the fact that Artaud had already been excluded from the group, and he got the police to come to the theatre. Breton's position gave rise to an increasing level of discontent, and he was reproached for his tyrannical treatment of the members of the group.

In 1929, *La Révolution surréaliste* published the second *Surrealist Manifesto*. Breton thought it was his duty to remind everyone else what the principles of Surrealism were and to purge it of everything that, from his point of view, was a betrayal. In response to this, his former friends published a stinging pamphlet under the same title as the one given to their pamphlet against Anatole France: "A Corpse". As a result of these political conflicts, by the 1930s the Surrealist movement had arrived at a state of bifurcation: on one side was Breton's group, which took a position of revolutionary engagement; on the other side were those artists who from the mid-1920s were providing a demonstration of Surrealism in the visual arts, and establishing its place within them.

Aside from the growing activity of the artists in Paris, Surrealist art was now in evidence beyond France's borders. In 1931, the first important Surrealism exhibition was held in the United States, with works shown by Dalí, de Chirico, Ernst, Masson, Picasso, Miró, and others. Personal exhibitions of the Surrealists came to various American cities. By the end of the 1930s, exhibitions of the Surrealists had covered the whole of Europe, reaching Belgium and Holland, Zürich, Copenhagen, Prague, and London. Japan and Latin America also received their fair share of Surrealism. In the 1940s, the activities of the Surrealists continued primarily in America where many of them had gone to escape World War II. In June 1947, the International Exhibition of Surrealism was held in Paris at the Galerie Maeght. It could truly be said that the visual art of Surrealism had conquered the whole world.

A moment in the history of art had probably come when art needed an influx of new forces. If the visual language of painting at the beginning of the 20th century, had been the focus of concern of Fauvism, Cubism and Futurism, of Matisse, Picasso and Kandinsky, the role of Dada's nihilism was to pave the way for Surrealism to explore a yet unknown territory: the unconscious.

◄ **Francis Picabia**,
The Cacodylic Eye, 1921.
Oil on canvas and photographic collage including postcards and various cuts of paper, 148.6 x 117.4 cm.
Centre Georges-Pompidou,
Musée national d'art moderne, Paris.

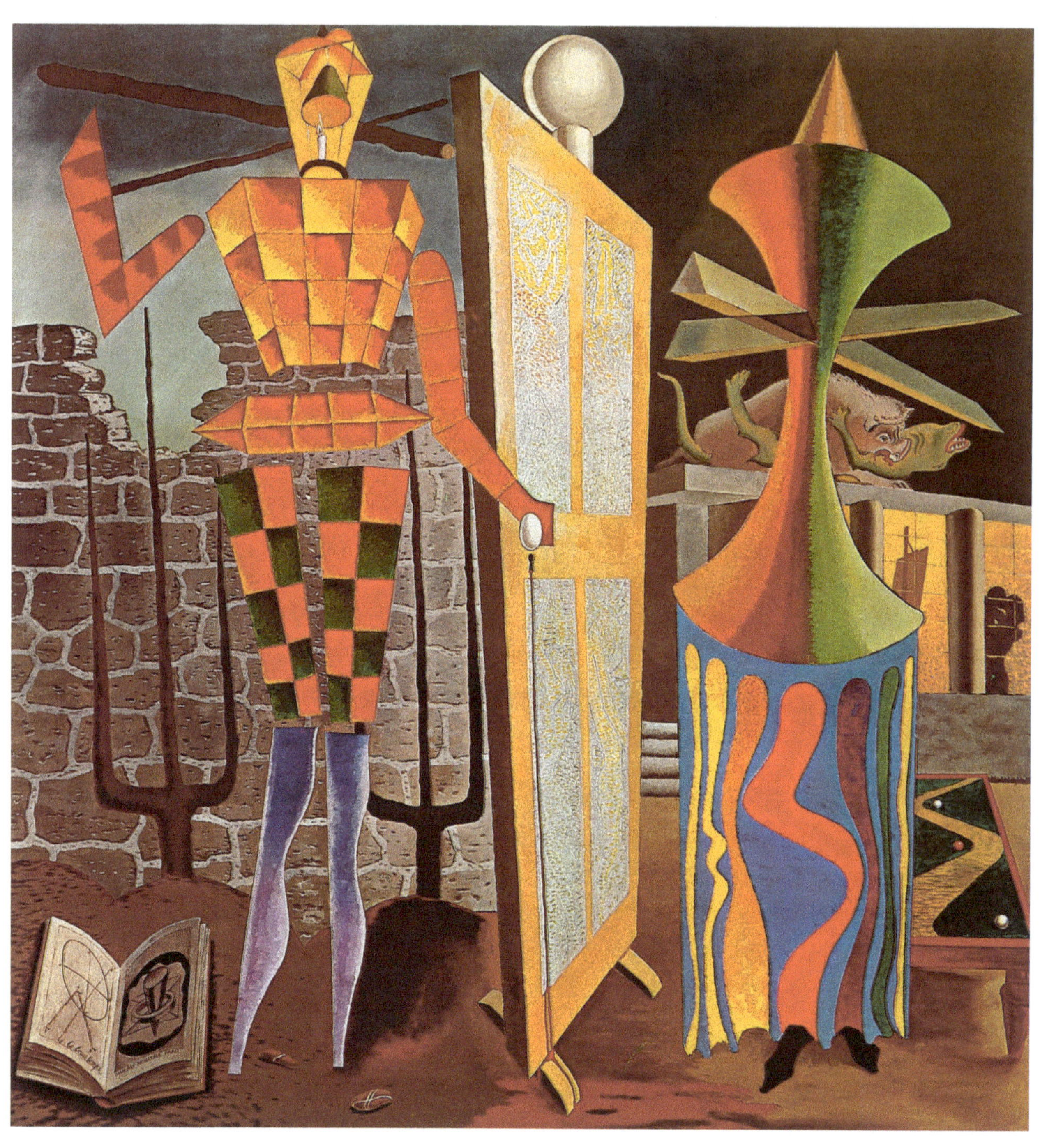

▲ **Man Ray (Emmanuel Radnitsky)**,
The Nice Weather, 1939. Private Collection.

MAJOR ARTISTS

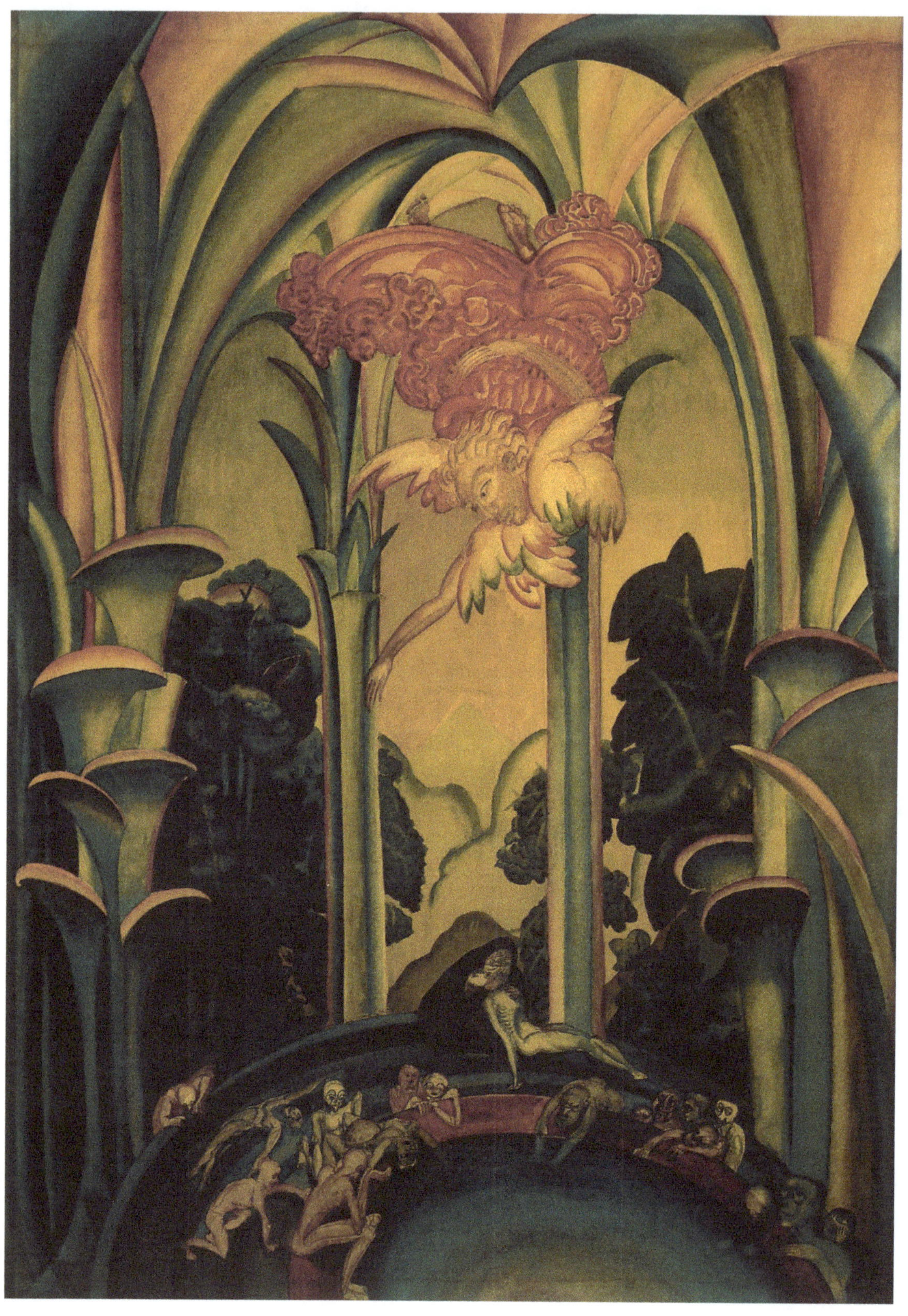

MAX ERNST

(Brühl 1891- Paris 1976)

In the world of painting created by Max Ernst, birds play a special role. Sometimes it is an inoffensive nightingale, which introduces unaccountable fear and panic into the life of the characters of the painting, and sometimes it is a menacing bird with the torso of a man and a spear in its hand. In the thicket of a forest, or in the outlines of figures can be discerned the features of the bird which obsessively haunted the artist all his life.

Ernst said that in his childhood he had a favourite pink parrot. One day in the morning, he found it lying dead in its cage. At that very moment he was told that his sister Apollonia – Loni – had been born during the night. The shock was so strong that the fifteen-year-old Max fainted. The bird acquired a mystical significance for him, it became the incarnation of the forces of life and death. Max called her Loplop, a sinister name in which there is also a note of irony.

◄ **Max Ernst**,
The Lake Bethesda, 1911.
Watercolour on cardboard, 53.5 x 42 cm.
Kasimir Hagen Collection, Kunstgewerbsmuseum, Cologne.

Maximilian Ernst was born on 2 April 1891, in the town of Brühl. Fate had ensured that his childhood was to be spent in a strange, surrealistic setting. Max's father, Philip Ernst, obtained the post of teacher in a school for the deaf and dumb. Max and his brothers and sisters grew up in an atmosphere of silence.

Max's taciturn, withdrawn father devoted the whole of his free time to painting. In his childhood he had already reached a point of perfection, which he had acquired by copying the pictures of the 19th century. He saw the collections of paintings in the Cologne Museum, and admired the fantasy of the masters of the 14th and 15th centuries and the romantic pictures of Caspar David Friedrich.

Max said that it was in fact after an exhibition that, bowled over by Picasso's painting, he finally decided to become an artist. In 1913, Max Ernst's own picture was exhibited in Berlin, at the first German Salon d'Automne. In the summer of 1914, the war betrayed all their dreams for the future.

In 1919, Max headed for Munich, and there he discovered Dadaist printed matter from Zürich, as well as the Italian journal *Valori plastici*, with

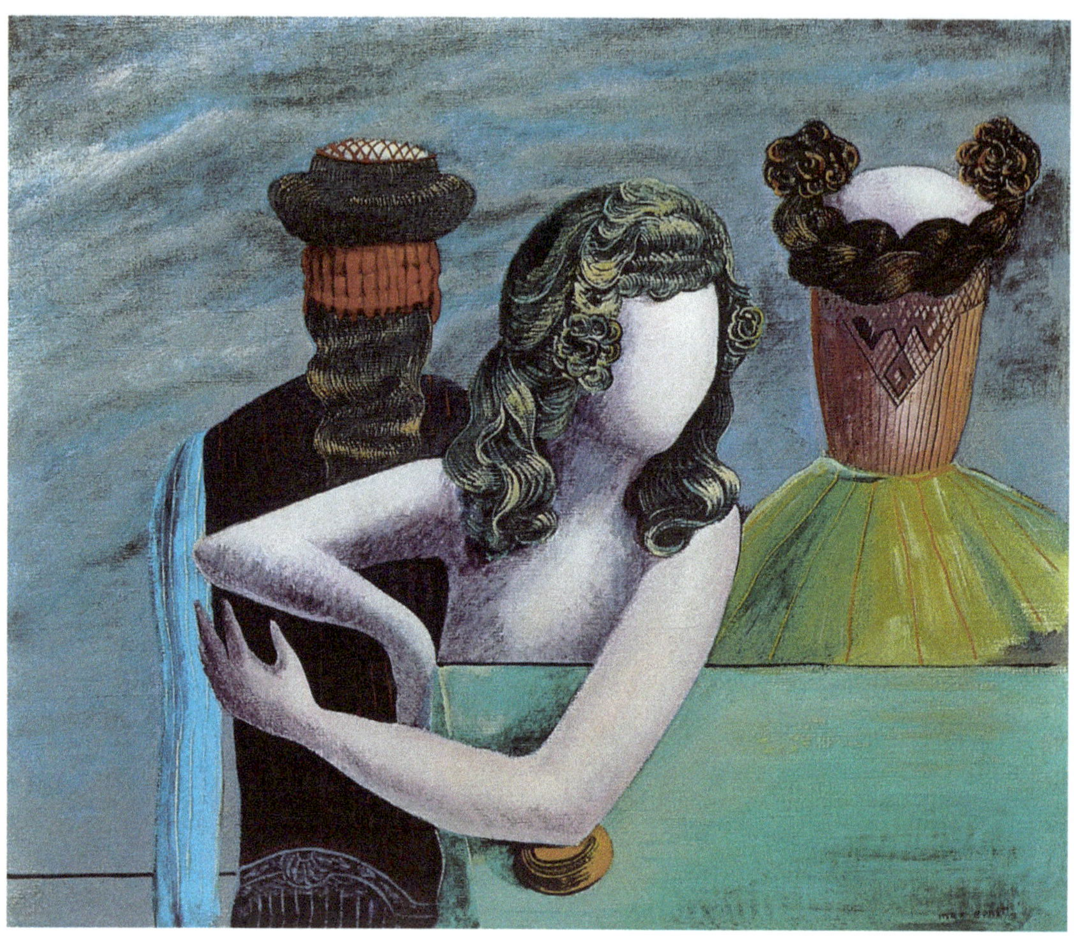

▲ **Max Ernst**,
The Sunday Guests, 1924.
Oil on canvas, 55 x 65 cm.
Private Collection.

Max Ernst, ▶
With the First Pure Word, 1923.
Oil on a plaster wall in the house of Paul Éluard in
Eaubonne, transferred on canvas, 232 x 167 cm.
Kunstsammlung Nordrhein-Westfalen, Düsseldorf.

reproductions of the paintings by Giorgio de Chirico; it had then published an album with eight lithographs in de Chirico's honour. The two things put together laid the foundations for Ernst's new aesthetic.

In the apparently frivolous circumstances of the Dadaist period, Max Ernst created his own special category of works – the collage. The collages of Picasso and the Cubists who surrounded him were pursuing the objective of creating purely visual works, and what interested them was form and volume. He used fragments of photographs, illustrations of books, and supplemented them with his own drawings or painterly elements.

The name represents an integral part of the composition. This name could be a word, a phrase, or a whole passage, and it was absolutely out

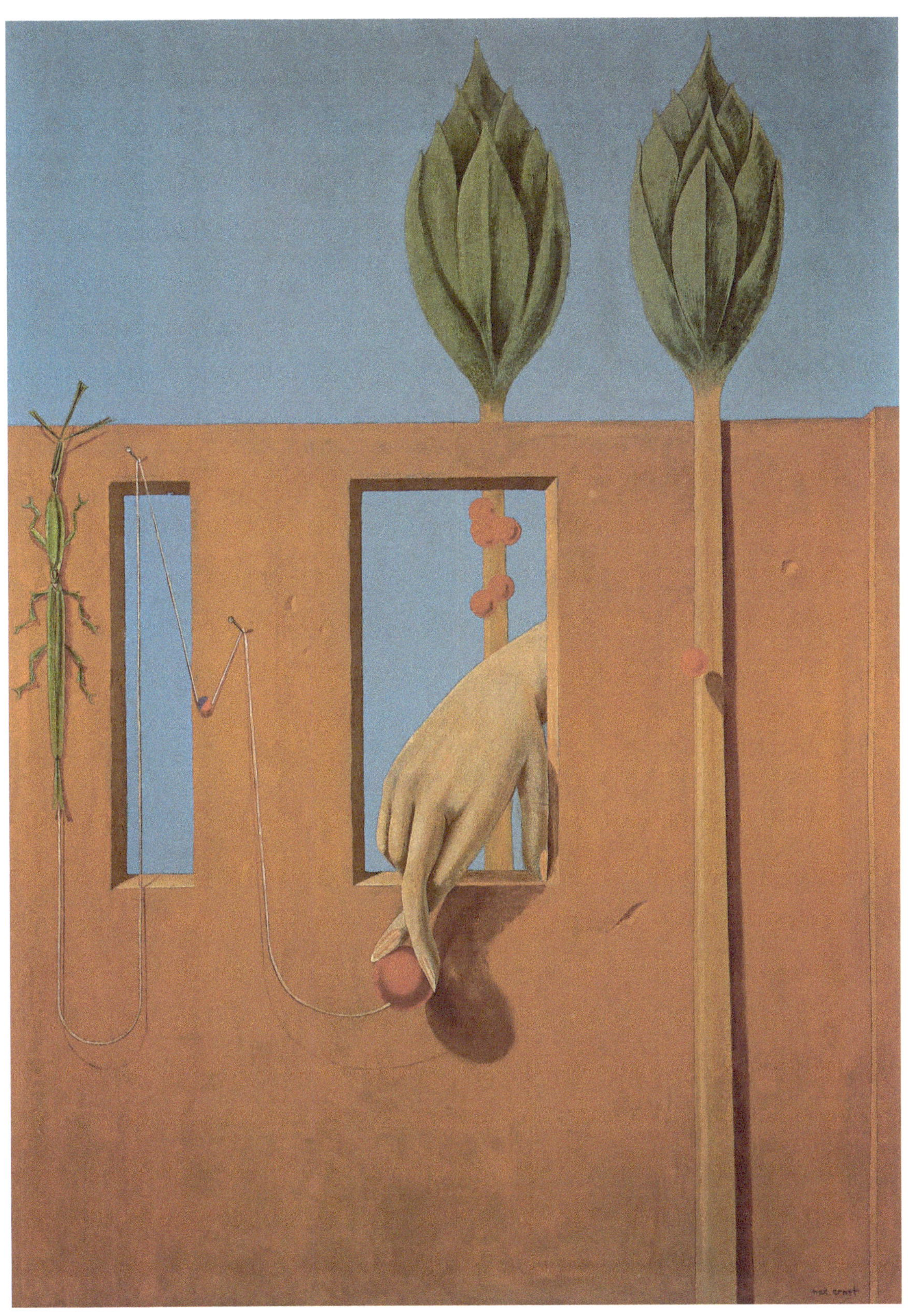

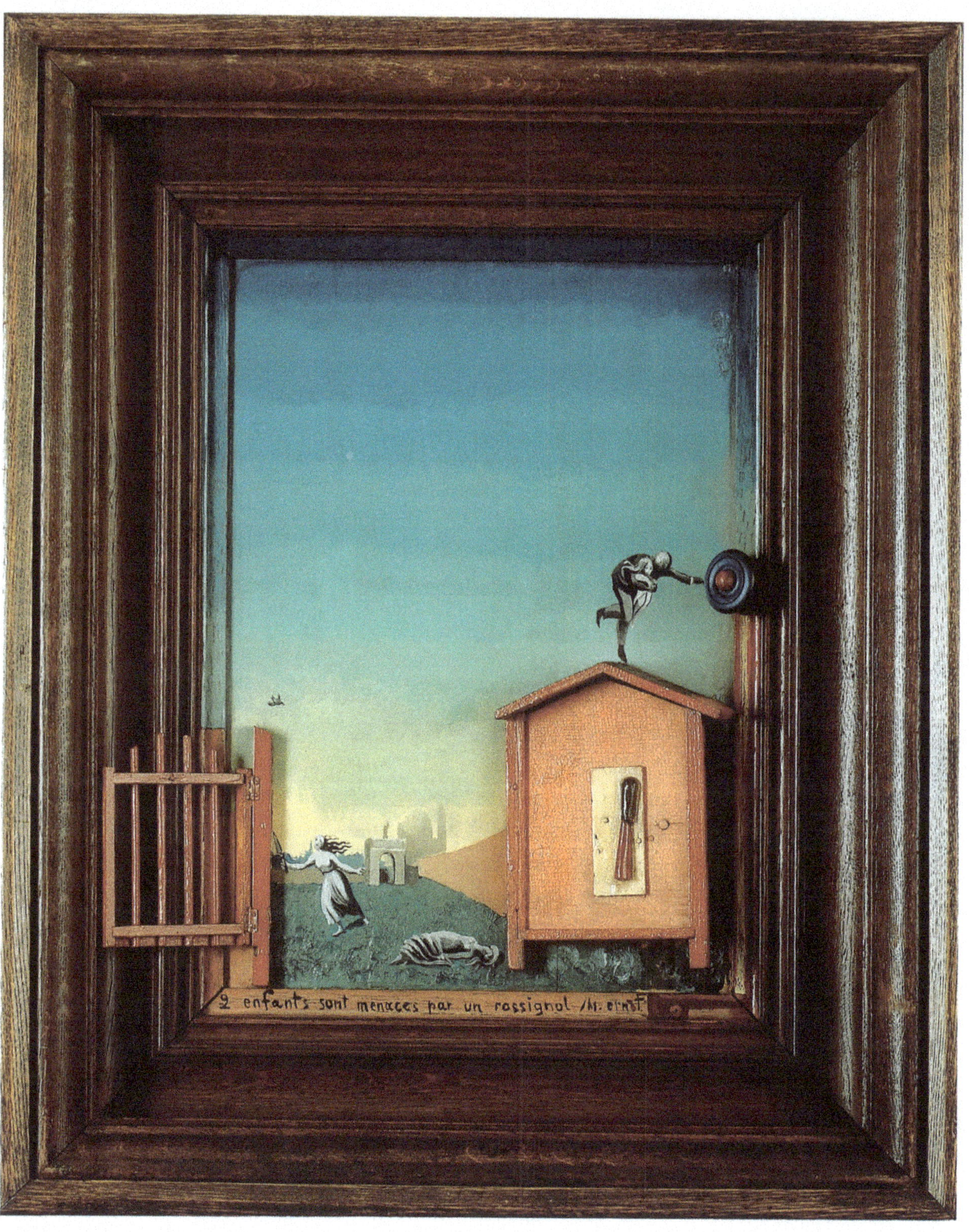
2 enfants sont menacés par un rossignol /M. ernst

of keeping with the image, but it constituted an independent poetic work in its own right. The collages were the origin of Ernst's work on the creation of the proper figurative language, which for painting could not be restricted by the same kind of automatism used in writing.

Éluard was the first buyer of Max's works. Éluard persuaded Max to move to Paris, and in the summer of 1922, he settled beside the Canal Saint-Martin. This year was notable for a documentary picture that is exceptional in Ernst's body of work, a portrait of the future Surrealists entitled *A Friends' Reunion*.

With this method, which he called "frottage" (from the word "to rub"), Max began to expose the designs of the veins on a leaf; the rough texture of a sack, the fibres with which rope is woven; the interlacing of the sticks from which a basket is made. According to him, he found the most varied images in the drawings he had obtained: the sea and the rain, human heads, animals, sphinxes, landscapes, a shawl with flowers and even Eve.

In the mid-1920s, Max Ernst took the place he deserved in the Surrealist group. The Paris galleries noticed Ernst and began to exhibit his work. He obtained recognition in the French provinces and abroad. The Belgian Surrealist René Magritte, who joined the group in 1927, admired his painting.

◀ **Max Ernst,**
Two Children are Threatened by a Nightingale, 1924.
Oil on wood with painted wood elements and frame,
69.8 x 57.1 x 11.4 cm.
The Museum of Modern Art, New York.

In December 1928, one of the most prestigious galleries in Paris, the Galerie Bernheim-Jeune, opened an exhibition entitled "Max Ernst, his birds, his new flowers, his flying forests, his curses, his demons." René Crevel wrote the catalogue text. The first buyers of Ernst's pictures made themselves known.

In 1929, he brought out his first album *The Hundred Headless Woman*. However, the first crack in his relationship with André Breton also dates from this period. Picasso brought Serge Diaghilev to Ernst's exhibition and advised him to commission scenery from Ernst and Miró for *Romeo and Juliet* in the production to be staged by Diaghilev's Ballets Russes.

Ernst's painting from the late 1930s and early 1940s is the work of a true visionary. After the forest, in his pictures there now appeared cities. The technique of "scratching" produced a striking effect. The woven texture that appeared on the canvas created the impression of stone blocks decorated by an ornamental design. In the picture which Ernst called *The Whole City*, an ancient pyramid rooted in the earth has become overgrown with the flowers and grasses which Ernst so loved to draw.

In 1936, the Spanish artist from the Canary Islands, Óscar Domínguez, invented one more means of automatic drawing – "decalcomania without a preconceived objective". Ernst used this method in oil painting. He laid thick paint directly onto the canvas. When the blob of paint was spread around, unforeseen images were obtained: human faces, plants, forests, cities and fabulous beasts. In Max's hands, one further method appeared: he now used not only the colour, but also the texture of the thick paint itself.

In 1939, Max Ernst, like all Germans in France, was immediately interned. The conditions of life in the prison of Largentière were difficult to bear. An appeal by Paul Éluard to the president enabled Ernst to be discharged from the camp. By Christmas, he had returned to his own village of Saint-Martin in Ardèche, but not for long. In May he was handcuffed and sent away to a camp in the Drome.

The most prophetic of his paintings of this period is undoubtedly *Europe After the Rain*. A landscape which was once made up of mountains, trees, and human habitations has been transformed into disfigured stones and fragments; there are birds everywhere, Loplop is triumphant. Max Ernst's painting had never until then attained such expressiveness and such pathos. It is not surprising that his painting should have impressed the American Peggy Guggenheim, who was quick to buy up everything he painted in these last years.

He met Peggy in Marseille where he had gone to organise his departure for America. In Marseille, the Surrealists – André Breton, Benjamin Peret, Óscar Domínguez, Marcel Duchamp, and many others – were awaiting the chance of a passage to America. On 14 July 1941 Ernst arrived in New York and soon afterwards married Peggy Guggenheim, from whom within a few months he was divorced.

In the years of World War II, it was actually possible to put together a presentation on the art of the European avant-garde in America. One of the New York galleries assembled in an exhibition the works of the most varied artists – Chagall, Ernst, Tanguy, Zadkine, Matta, Léger, Breton, Mondrian, Masson, and others. When combined, they formed a striking panorama of the diversity of modern art.

In America, Max Ernst met the young artist Dorothea Tanning, whose painting impressed him by the way it corresponded to what the European Surrealists were doing. She soon became his wife. In 1946, Ernst and Dorothea settled in on the edge of forests and desert in Sedona, Arizona. He discovered the art of the American Indians.

In the 1940s, geometric motifs appeared in his pictures and they accorded harmoniously with the world of natural history. *Cocktail Drinker* and *Euclid* were painted in 1945. There was a period when tiny pictures appeared in Max's paintings, at times the size of a postage stamp; he called them "The Microbes". In 1948, he received American citizenship. For both of them, Max and Dorothea, this was an extraordinarily productive time.

In 1953, Max and Dorothea returned to France. In 1954, he obtained the grand prize at the Venice Biennale, and was immediately excluded from the Surrealist group: they were against all official awards. However, by this time Max was one of the greatest painting masters in Europe. The house in Ardèche was sold, and Max and Dorothea settled in the vicinity of Chinon. Max Ernst worked there until his death in 1976.

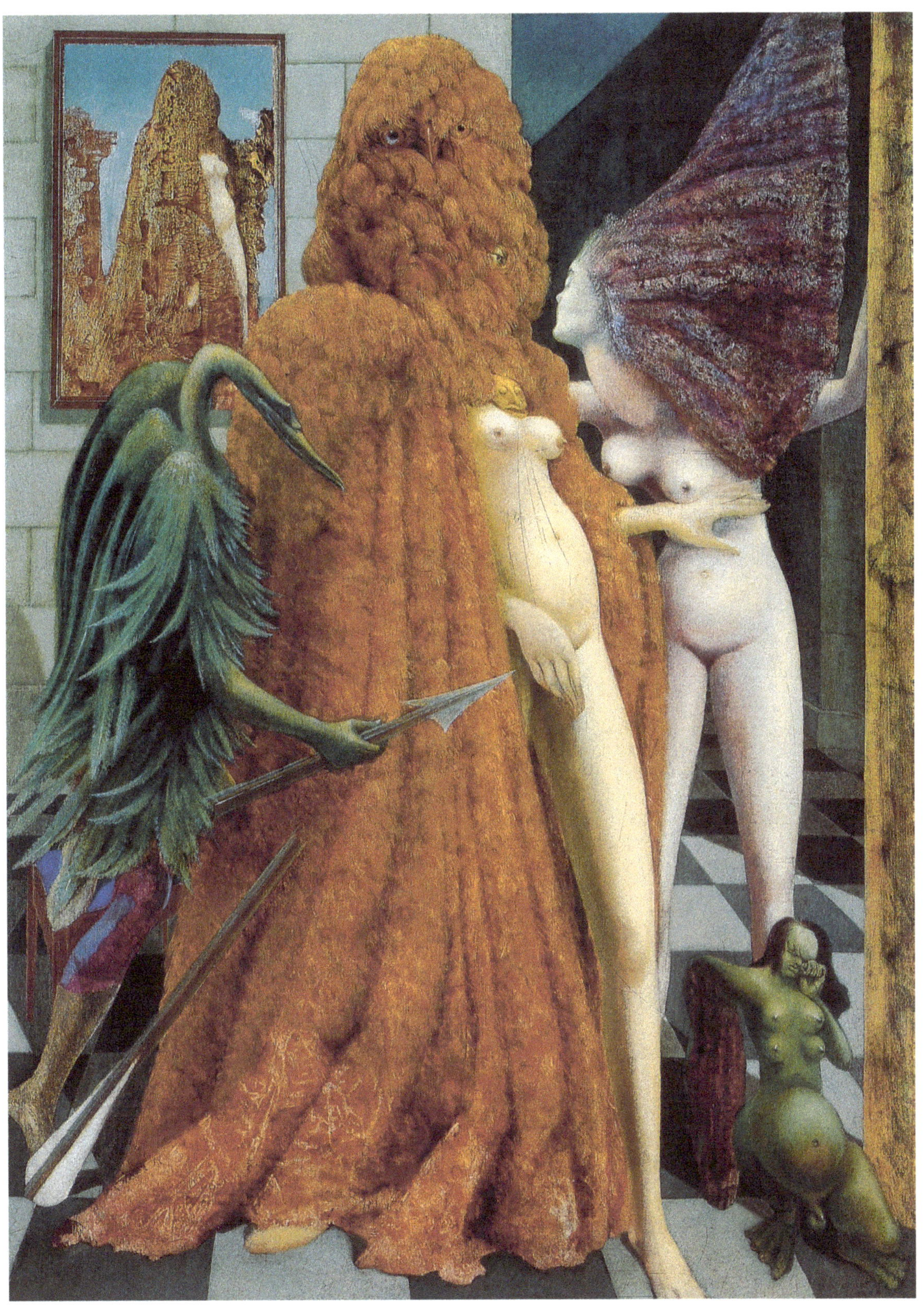

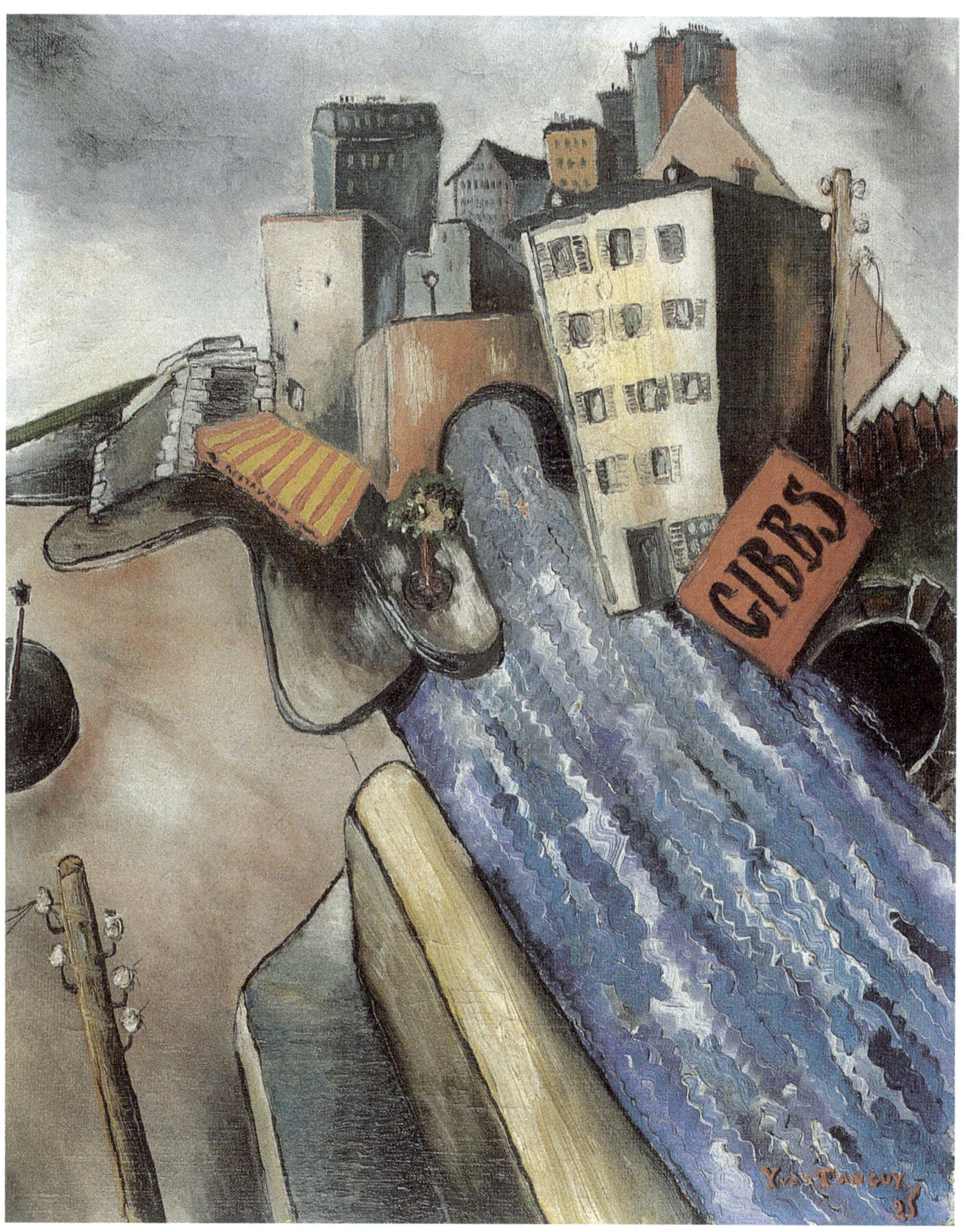
RESTAVRANT
GIBBS
Yves Tanguy
25

YVES TANGUY

(1900 Paris - Woodbury, Connecticut 1955)

Yves Tanguy entered Surrealism without getting involved in Dada. André Breton was amazed at the sight of Tanguy and his friends' house in Paris. It was a Surrealist house, in which everything was made by Tanguy's hands. He said that he took up painting as a result of the impression made on him by an encounter with a picture of Giorgio de Chirico. However, direct influences of de Chirico can never be detected anywhere.

Yves Tanguy was born on 5 January 1900 in Paris. Yves's father, Felix Tanguy, was a captain who made long voyages. His family lived in the Naval Ministry on the Place de la Concorde. By a quirk of fate, he found himself at the lycée in the same class as Pierre Matisse, who brought Yves to the studio of his father, Henri Matisse. Matisse's painting made a huge impression on the fourteen-year-old Yves; this was the first time he had come into close contact with art. In 1912, Yves's mother bought an old-fashioned house in Brittany which dated to the 16th century. The village had its own naïve painter who painted rural scenes which he sold to tourists. His work attracted Yves's interest. It may be that it was here that he began to draw.

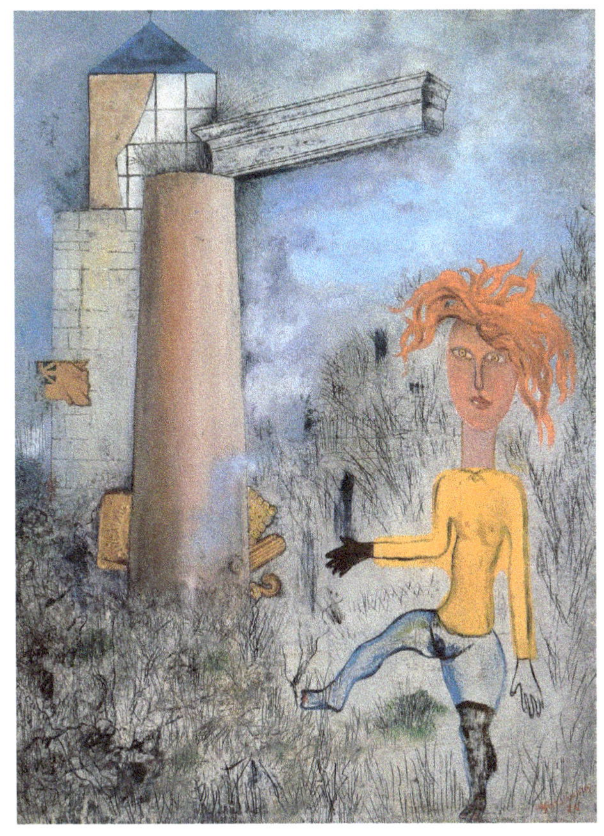

▲ **Yves Tanguy,**
The Girl with Red Hair, 1926.
Oil on canvas, 61 x 46.2 cm.
Jacqueline Matisse-Monnier Collection.

◀ **Yves Tanguy,**
The Bridge, 1925.
Oil on canvas, 40 x 33 cm.
National Gallery of Art, Washington, D. C.

In 1914, Yves Tanguy was only fourteen. He spent the duration of the war in Paris, under the care of his elder sister. According to his own recollections, he got to know the life of Paris's lower depths, drugs, prostitution, and vagrancy. This period came to an end in 1918, when Yves joined the merchant navy. Life itself seemed to have given him the opportunity to see the most varied and fabulous natural scenery. As well as European countries, he saw Argentina, Brazil and North Africa.

After he was demobilised in 1922, Tanguy returned to Paris and met up with Jacques Prévert who introduced Yves to his brother Pierre, and his friend from military service, Marcel Duhamel. Things really were looking up for them: Marcel Duhamel was a man of means and managed the hotel Grosvenor which belonged to his uncle. Duhamel rented a house, a former shop, in the Montparnasse District. They all made their home there together. This was a period of avid absorption in Parisian life for Tanguy and his friends. They were drawn to everything related to the world at the margins of society.

In 1924, they read the *Surrealist Manifesto* and the first number of *La Révolution surréaliste*. In November 1925, Yves Tanguy saw the Surrealist painting exhibition organised by the Galerie Pierre, where works by de Chirico, Arp, Ernst, Klee, Masson, Miró, and Picasso were shown. His friends said that afterwards, he destroyed everything that he had painted earlier.

In these years Tanguy painted strange landscapes. In them the buildings of Paris and Nantes are sometimes confused, sometimes only one brick tower looms up against the background of a starry night. But in every landscape there was invariably an expanse that recedes into the distance, and a sense of the horizon, even when the line of the horizon was not drawn (*Dancing; Untitled*).

In the mid-1920s, Yves Tanguy tried out all the Surrealist work methods: he used rubbing, scratching and collage, and he began to make drawings using the automatic method. He drew in pencil, Indian ink and watercolour, combining drawing with collage. The combination of techniques produced striking results. In 1926, he made in Brittany a large composition on canvas in which he combined oil painting, pencil-drawing and collage *The Lamb of Invisibility*. None of Tanguy's drawings completed in Brittany have survived.

Tanguys' pictures bore strange titles: *Their White Belly Had Struck Me, Dung on the Left, Violets on the Right, Finish What I Started, I Have Come as I Had Promised. Farewell* and *Mama, Papa is Wounded!* (p. 97). At this point, Tanguy was inspired by his contact with the Surrealists and enthusiastic about their concepts. With Breton's help, he took many titles from psychiatry textbooks.

Yves Tanguy, ▶
Mama, Papa Is Wounded!, 1927.
Oil on canvas, 92.1 x 73 cm.
The Museum of Modern Art, New York.

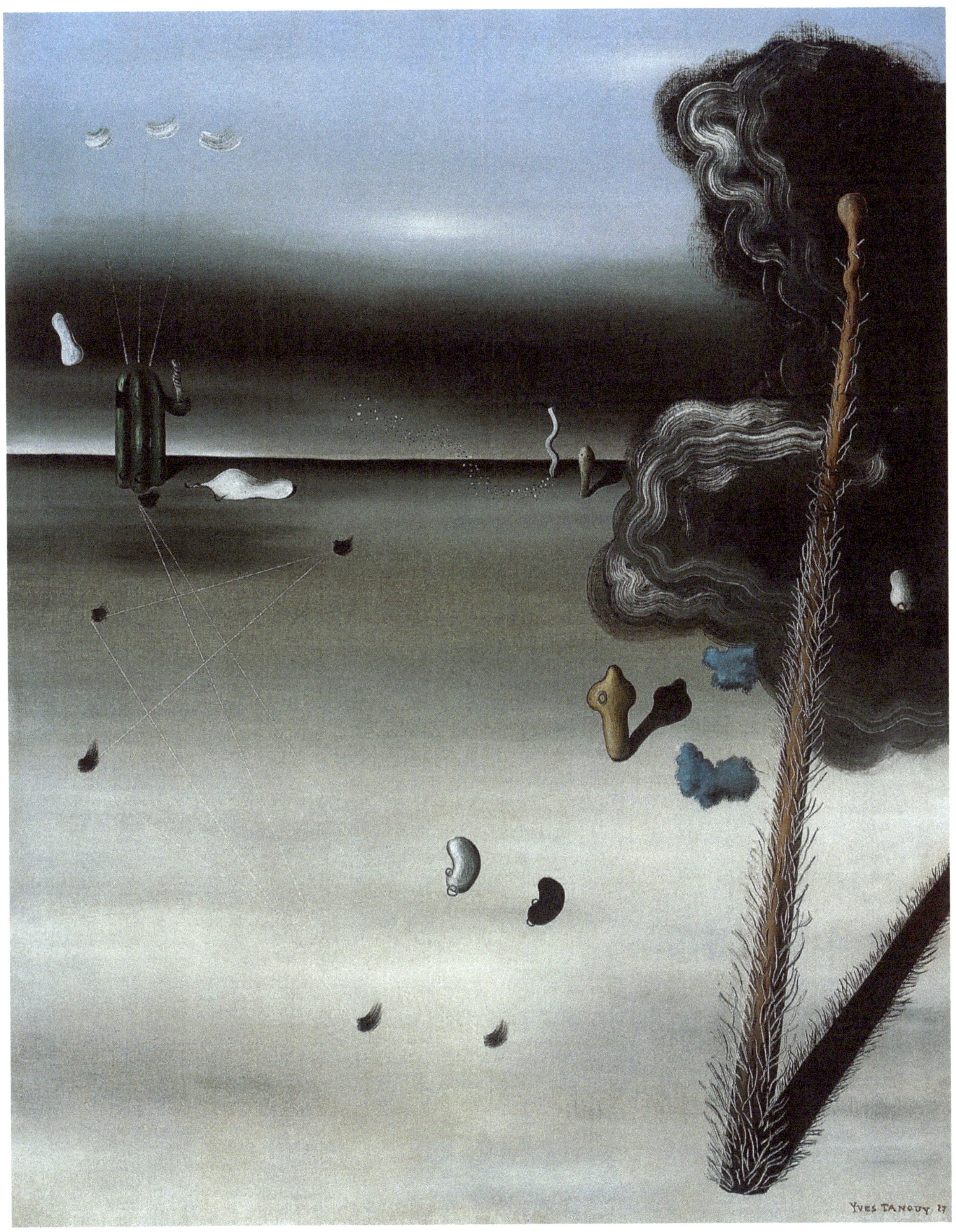

YVES TANGUY 27

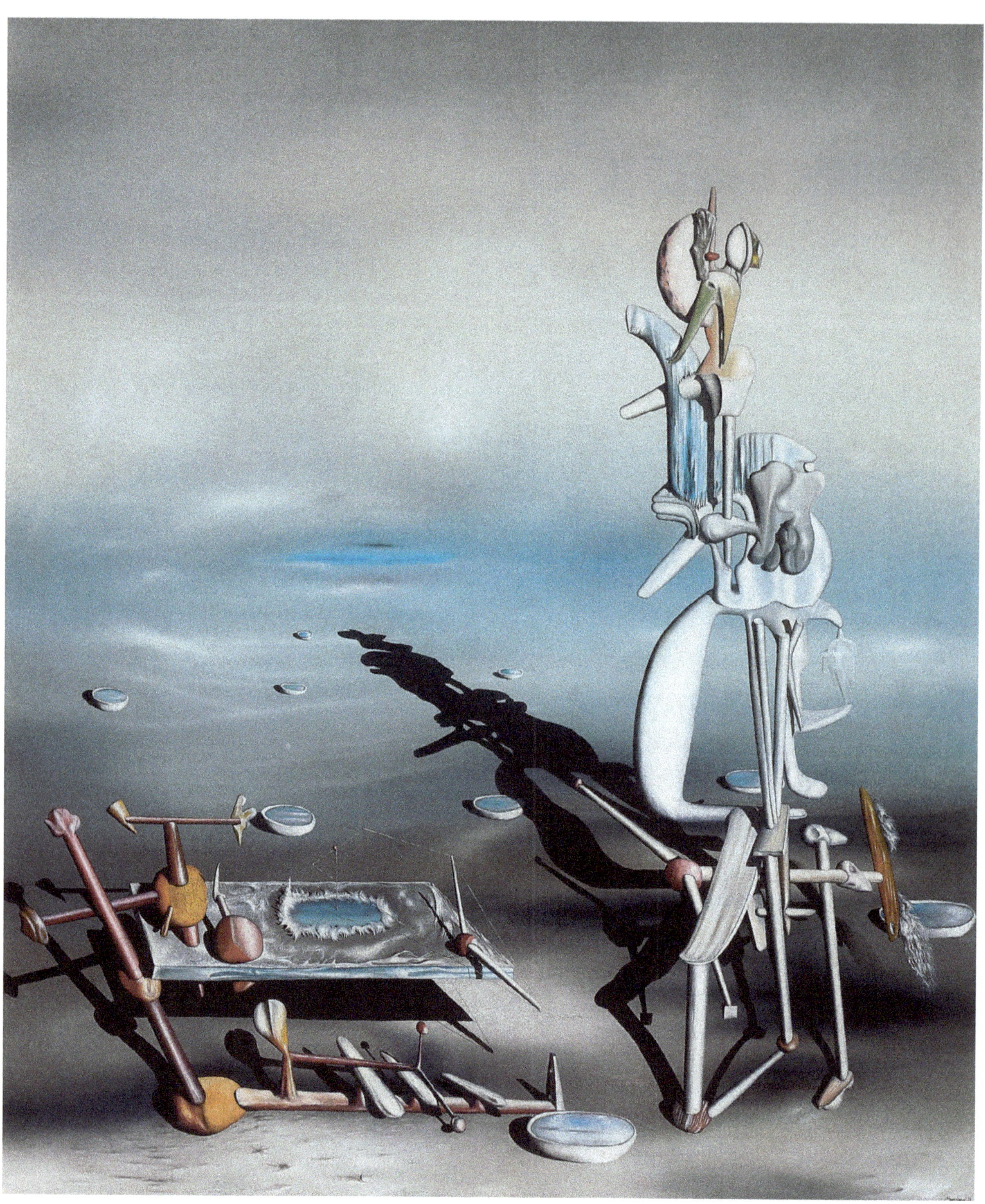

Mama, Papa is Wounded is one of Tanguy's most impressive pictures. In it there is everything that he found in his fantasy world up until then: a flat plain, the line of the horizon, small, indefinable objects or creatures. However, the combination of objects and space creates an entirely new impression.

The 1930s brought Yves Tanguy wide recognition. In addition to personal exhibitions in the galleries of Paris, he contributed to all the Surrealists' exhibitions, his pictures, collages, objects and drawings appeared in England, Belgium, Japan, New York, and Tenerife. In the period between the two wars, Yves Tanguy's work also became widely known in the United States. In November 1939, following the declaration of war, Yves Tanguy left for America.

In New York, Tanguy encountered the American artist Kay Sage. They had already met in France. Kay was involved in helping those artists who had remained in Europe during the war. In 1940, she became Tanguy's wife, and from that point on she was his lifelong companion. As soon as Tanguy had arrived in New York in December 1939, his former lycée classmate, Pierre Matisse, organised an exhibition of Tanguy's work in his gallery. In 1941, Tanguy's pictures were shown in the International Exhibition of Surrealism in Mexico organised by Breton. On 24 October 1942, Art of this Century,

◀ **Yves Tanguy**,
Indefinite Divisibility, 1942.
Oil on canvas, 101.6 x 88.9 cm.
Albright-Knox Art Gallery, Buffalo.

Peggy Guggenheim's New York gallery, opened and here Tanguy's pictures were also shown.

Tanguy's fame in America brought him sharply into conflict with André Breton. In 1945, at the time of one of Tanguy's exhibitions at the Matisse gallery, Breton criticised Tanguy for his "embourgeoisement" and suggested that Matisse should break off his contract with him. Max Ernst rallied fiercely in Yves Tanguy's defence. In 1948, he obtained American citizenship. When he returned to Paris, he saw all his old friends, apart from Breton. He could not resist going to see Locronan one last time, before leaving France for good.

It seems that towards the end of his life, Tanguy became accustomed to this world, which ceased to be mysterious for him. (*Time, a Mirage*). But even if the elements of which it consisted may have been incomprehensible, they are still real, solid and substantial, and they have form and volume (*Imaginary Numbers*).

At the end of his life, Tanguy painted a huge picture on which, in his own words, he worked eight or nine hours a day over the course of five weeks. Here, there was everything that could be seen in his pictures before: the plain, the clouded sky, the line of the horizon. Only now the plain is so crowded that no place on it is left empty (*Multiplication of Arcs*).

Yves Tanguy died on 15 January 1955 on his farm in America. In accordance with his will, Pierre Matisse scattered his ashes over the Douarnenez Bay in Brittany.

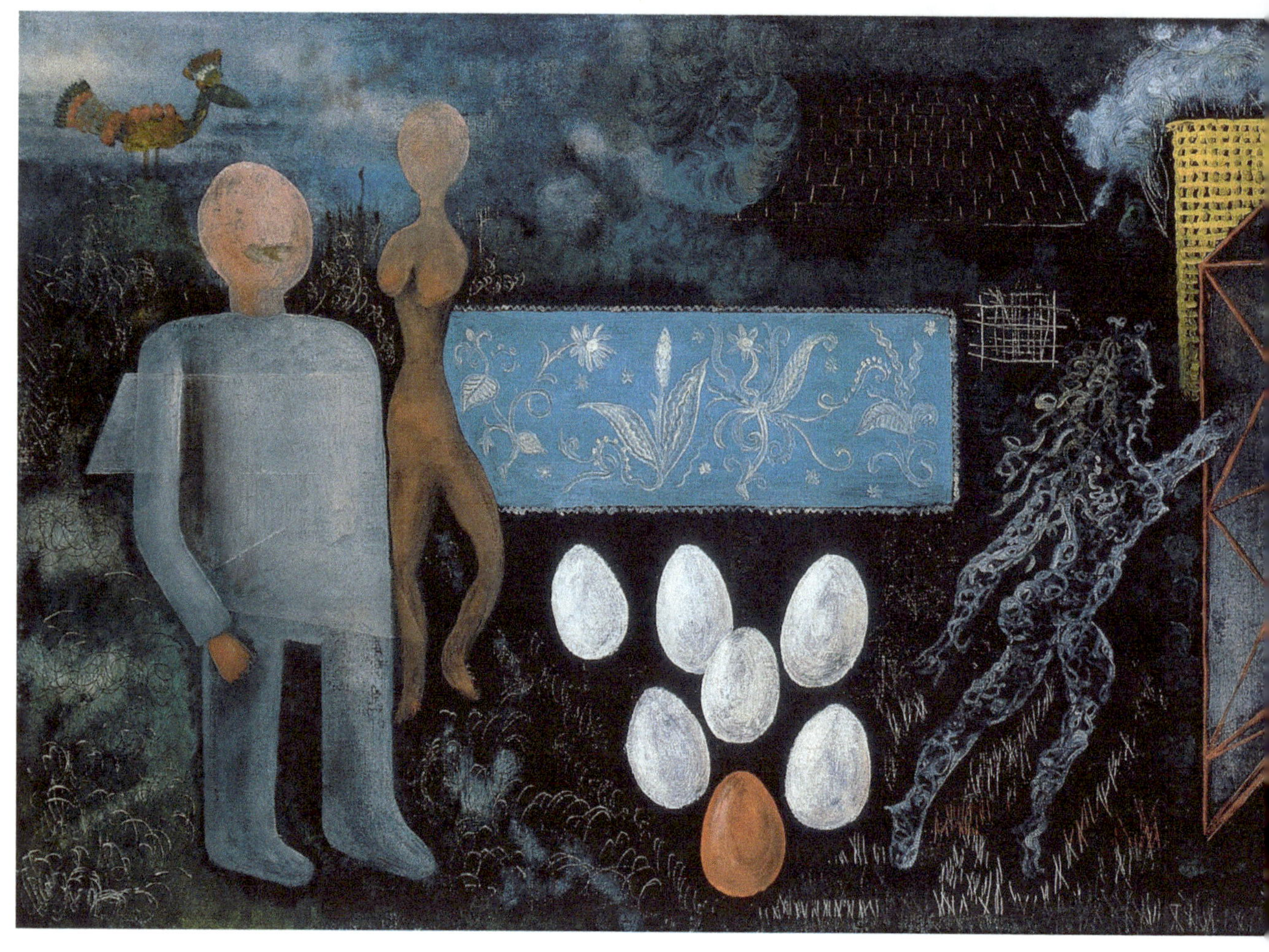

▲ **Yves Tanguy**,
Fantômas, 1925-1926.
Oil on canvas, 50 x 149.5 cm.
Pierre and Maria-Gaetana Matisse Foundation Collection,
New York.

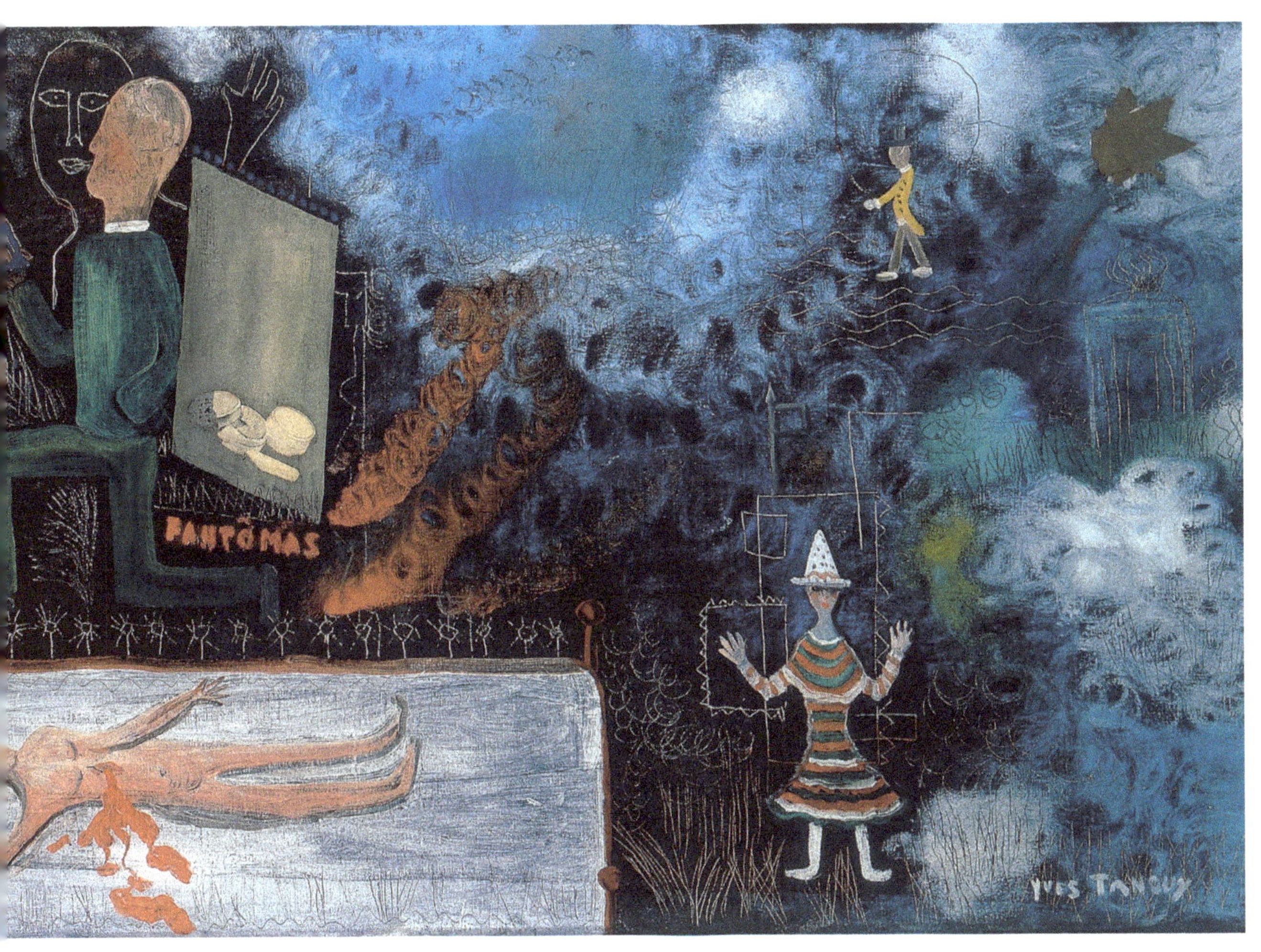

PANTOMAS
YVES TANGUY

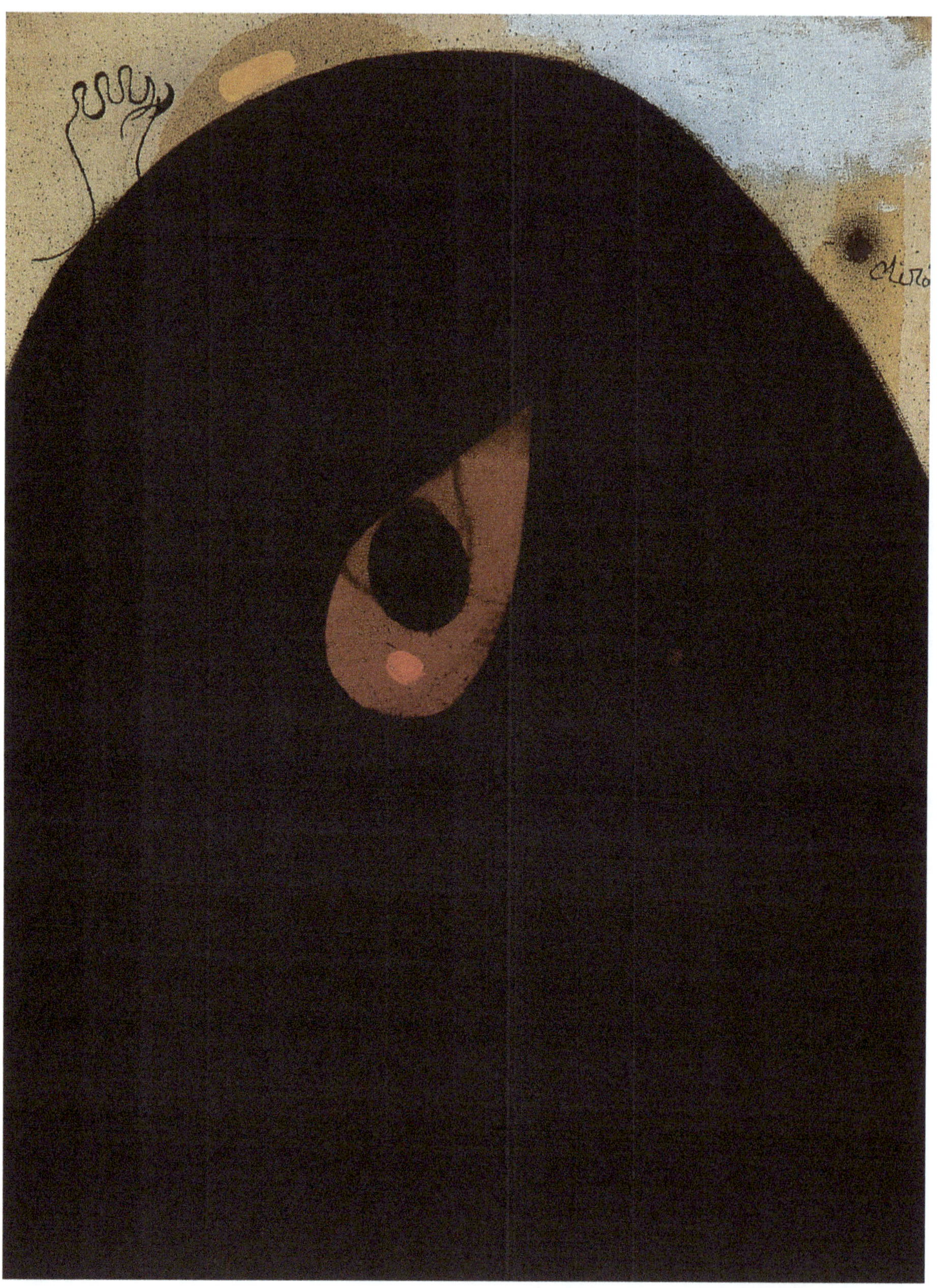

JOAN MIRÓ

(1893 Barcelona– 1983 Palma de Mallorca)

Joan Miró loved Catalonia. All his life he painted its dazzling blue sky. It is difficult to say whether, in the body of work Miró has left us, there is even one picture without the sun. Wherever he worked, whether in a Paris studio or on the island of Majorca, the colour and light of Catalonia always remained in his painting. It was light, colourful and transparent. Miró did not come to Surrealism by accident. Everything he created is a dream. Sometimes it is incomprehensible and disturbing, like any dream. But more often it is happy, with childlike purity and naivety.

Joan Miró was born on 20 April 1893 in Barcelona. He was the first-born child of Miguel Miró Adzerias, a goldsmith and watchmaker, and Dolores Ferra, daughter of a cabinet-maker from the island of Majorca. In his family, where fine and serious work was appreciated more than anything, he acquired the skills of a craftsman and the habit of going deeply into a problem in order to find the right solution to it.

◀ **Joan Miró**,
Head, 1974.
Acrylic paint on canvas, 65.1 x 50 cm.
Fundació Joan Miró, Barcelona.

His parents sent him to commercial school, but he put all his effort into his drawing at the art school in Lonja. When he reached the age of seventeen, his parents insisted that he should work in the Barcelona trading firm of Dalmau Oliveras. Miró was obliged to abandon art school. When he became seriously ill, his parents sent him to their house in Montroig, where he was able to devote himself completely to painting. In 1912, Miró enrolled at the Escola d'Arte de Francisco Gali in Barcelona, and simultaneously studied at the Académie libre du dessin du Cercle Saint Luc. Miró met Picabia, saw his painting, and became familiar with the Dadaist journal *391*. The influence of Cézanne, Van Gogh, and Matisse can be felt in Miró's paintings from this time.

After the failure of his first individual exhibition at the Galerie Dalmau in Barcelona, Miró settled in Montroig, where a new language began to develop in his painting. Now it was as though Miró was examining everything around him under a microscope. He painted farms, fields, and kitchen-gardens, depicting each little ridge and each blade of grass with a peasant's love and a miniaturist's care – the "detailist" period in his work had begun (*The Farm*).

In the spring of 1919, Miró travelled to Paris for the first time where he immediately became friends with another artist from Barcelona, Pablo Picasso. Much later, Miró would introduce Salvador Dalí to Picasso and draw the young Catalan into the circle of the Paris Surrealists. Picasso insisted that Miró give him the self-portrait he had just painted (*Self-Portrait*).

In summer, in Spain, he painted several landscapes of Montroig and the wonderful *Nude with Mirror*. The brightly coloured butterflies embroidered on the seat fabric might have come straight out of folk art. After this picture, there followed still lifes. (*The Table* (*Still Life with a Rabbit*), *Glove on a Table*; *Grain of Wheat*, *Gas Lamp*).

In 1920, together with André Masson, Miró rented a studio in Paris, an address which became one of the Surrealists' favourite haunts. However, he could not live without Catalonia, and every summer he went back to Montroig. Miró called himself an "international Catalan". In 1921, his first exhibition in Paris was held at the Galerie la Licorne. In 1923, Joan Miró painted his first surrealist picture – *The Tilled Field*, and following that, *The Hunter*.

Between 1925 and 1927, Miró worked under the enormous impact of the theory of automatic drawing. In 1924, he painted *Harlequin's Carnival*. It was an explosion of childlike raptures before all the beauty and variety of the world. At its centre was a spot of beautiful, dazzling light-blue colour, and around it, like a garland, was wound the inscription, which Miró had put into calligraphy: "This is the colour of my dream." This picture became something akin to Miró's own manifesto.

The delicate line, as naïve as is Miró's colour, introduced a touching fragility into his painting (*Composition with a Bird*). Often the artist's inscription became a graphic element of the picture. It added both to the decorative resonance and the interpretative possibilities of the picture (*A Big Crowd*).

In 1928, an exhibition of Miró's painting from 1926 and 1927 was held at the Georges Bernheim gallery on the Rue du Faubourg Saint-Honoré. In 1929, Miró married Pilar Juncosa, a girl who came from an old Majorca family. In 1930, Miró's individual exhibition in Paris at the Galerie Pierre offered examples of a new aspect to his work – paper collages. In the same year he had his first New York exhibition.

In 1933, Miró and his family were obliged to spend the whole year in Barcelona as a result of financial difficulties. By that time, his paintings reached a harmony, to the point where he found the strength to make the transition to monumental works. Later, in 1937, he completed a painting for the Spanish Pavilion of the International Exhibition in Paris, and later still, painted murals in Cincinatti,

Joan Miró, ▶
The Table (Still Life with Rabbit), 1920.
Oil on canvas, 130 x 110 cm.
Private Collection.

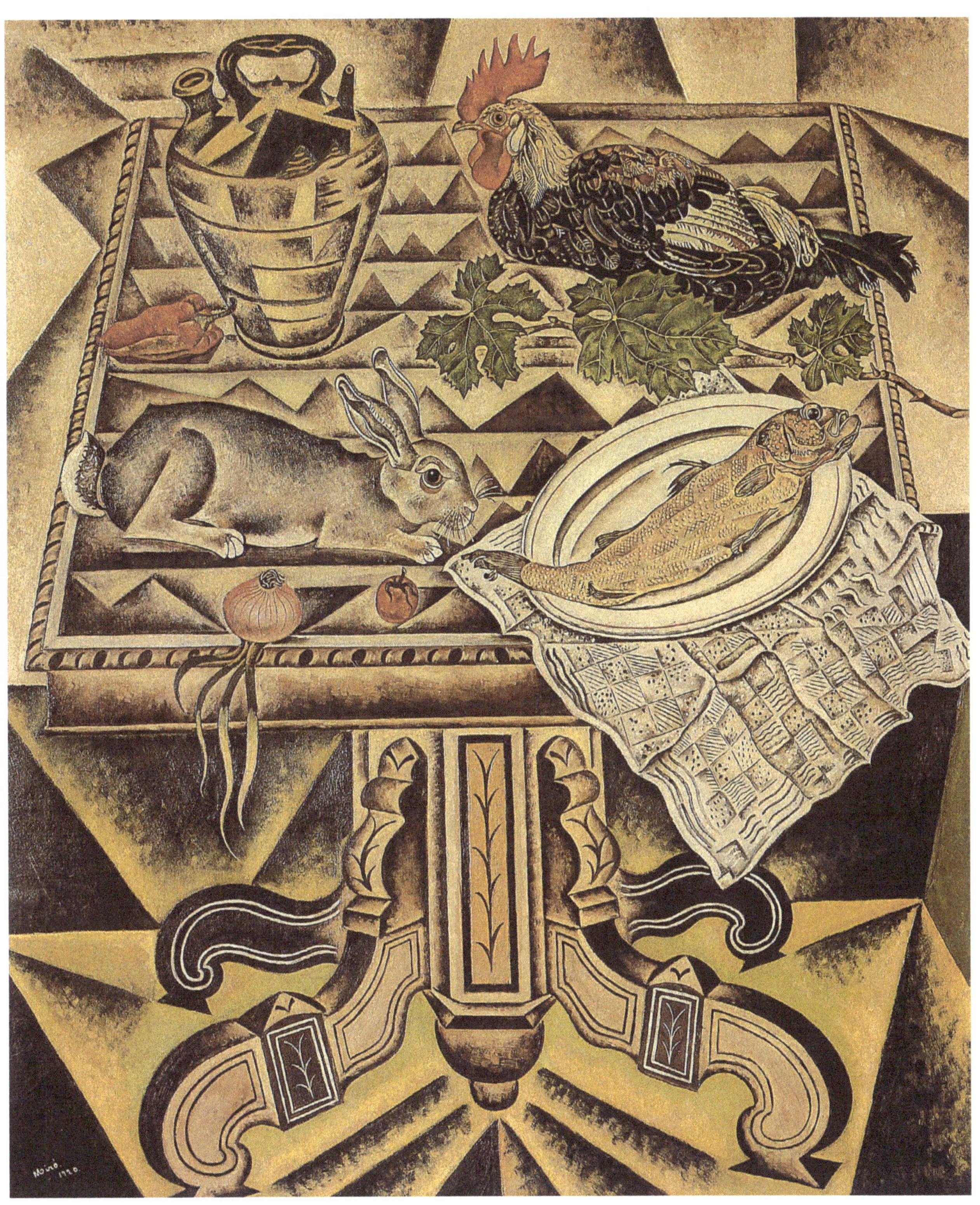

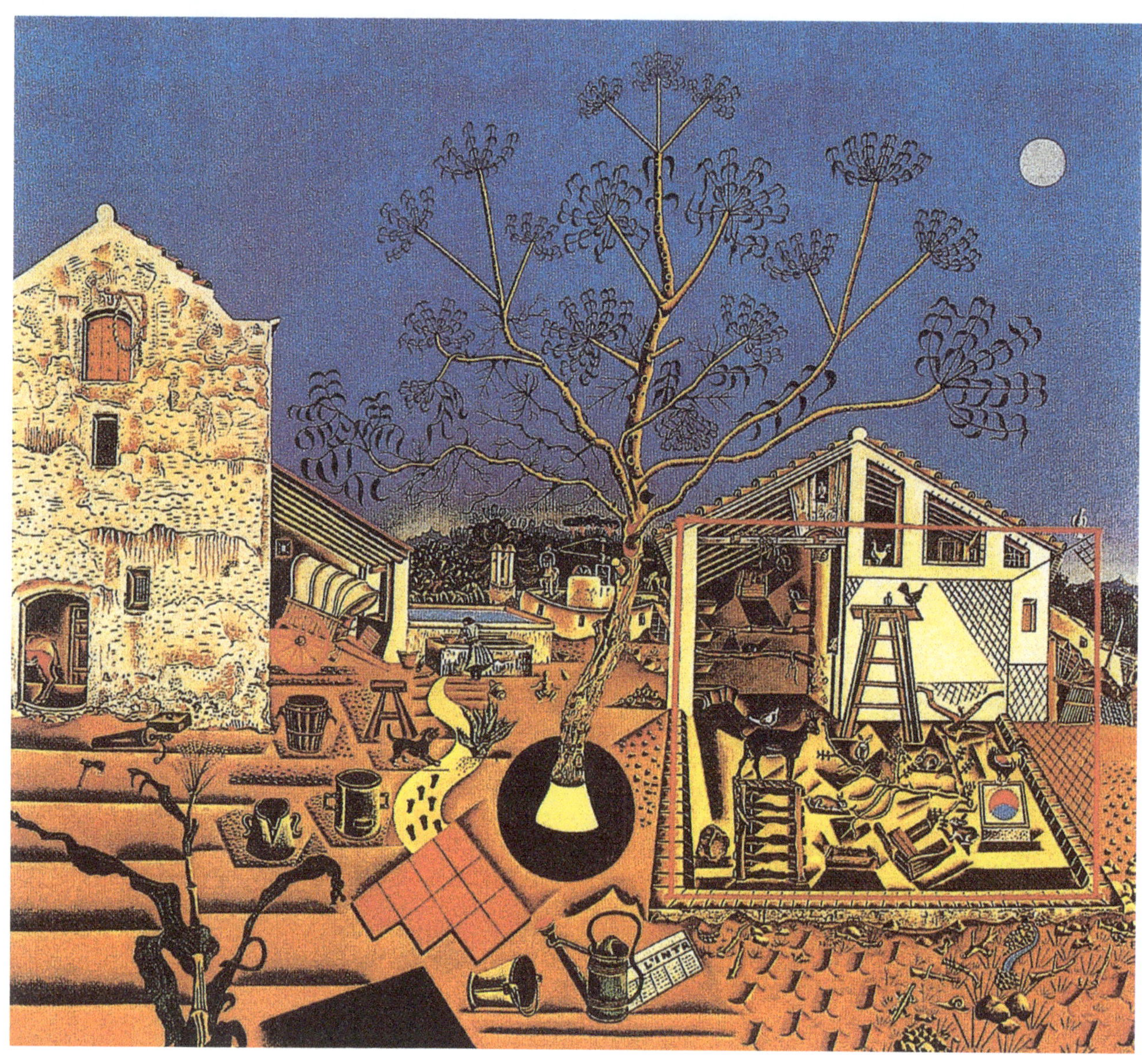

▲ **Joan Miró**,
The Farm, 1921-1922.
Oil on canvas, 123.8 x 141.3 x 3.3 cm.
National Gallery of Art, Washington, D. C.

Joan Miró, ▶
The Tilled Field, 1923-1924.
Oil on canvas, 66 x 92.7 cm.
Solomon R. Guggenheim Museum, New York.

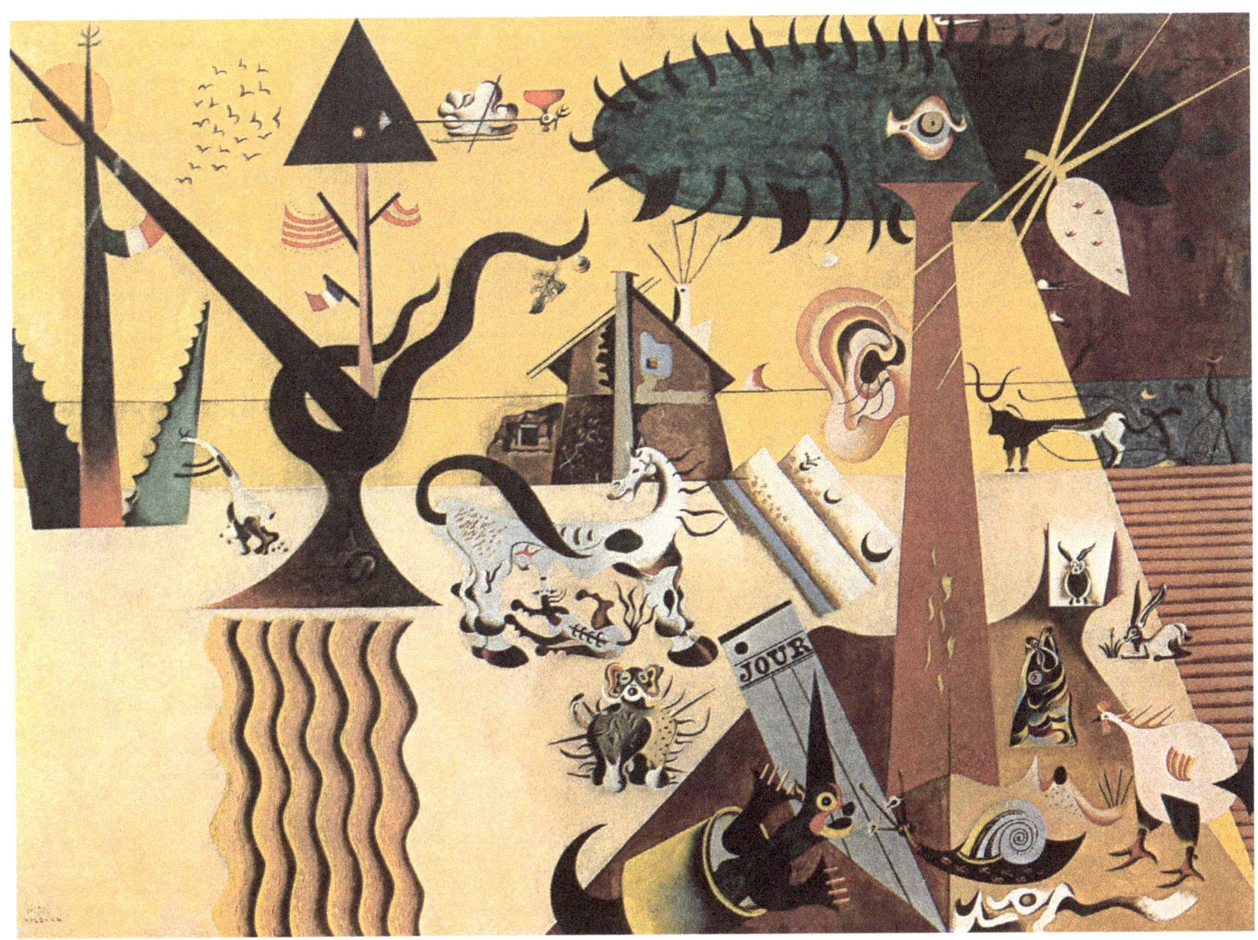

at Harvard, in New York in 1953, and finally, over 1957 and 1958, his masterpiece, *Walls of the Sun and the Moon*, for the UNESCO building in Paris.

In the spring of 1934, he completed sixteen large pastels which he himself called his "wild paintings". In Germany, Fascism was already triumphant. Miró managed to go to Berlin, where he stayed briefly and saw the work of those German artists whose paintings, by then, were no longer being shown. The situation in Spain was about to catch fire since the Civil War was just beginning.

The beginning of the world war found Miró in Varengeville, where Queneau, Braque, and Calder were then living. Miró continued to work. In the war years, he made endless compositions in gouache, pastel and oils, and depicted the stars, women and birds. But the night in his pictures lost its fairy-tale spirit, and the stars twinkled sadly. On May 20, 1940 they fled the invading German forces, first to Paris and then to Spain.

In 1939, Miró painted decorative canvases with a great number of figures. The precise line of the drawing outlines the contours of birds, jellyfish, strange little figures, and a human eye. Sometimes they bear titles which to him were traditional – *Figures and Birds in the Night*.

From the first days of the war, Miró had started to work on a large series of gouaches entitled *Constellations*. On the sheets of paper, the sun, the moon, and a large number of red and black stars make up the constellation designs. Miró began to work in ceramics and in 1945, his ceramics and sculpture in terracotta were shown for the first time in New York at Pierre Matisse's, and had a great success. He made his vases and plates with the skill of a genuine craftsman. However, each object was individual and impossible to recreate.

Miró's post-war period began with a series of large canvases – *Women and Bird in the Night*. Most often, the language of a line against a bright background with a few spots of colour is predominant in them (*Woman Dreaming of Escape*). He was still living in Barcelona. He enjoyed any news of the Paris art world – under Franco in Spain, artists were virtually isolated from the outside world.

In 1947, he travelled for the first time to the United States, where he was already well-known. He worked there on an enormous mural, 2 m by 10 m, for the Terrace Hilton Hotel in Cincinnati. In the spring of 1948, after an absence of eight years, Miró returned to Paris. In his individual exhibition at the Galerie Maeght, eighty-eight paintings and ceramics pieces appeared. In 1949, his exhibitions came to Barcelona, the Berne Kunsthalle and Basel. At the age of fifty, Joan Miró had attained worldwide recognition.

His pictures fascinate as much as ever; they remain poems in colours, enigmatic and appealing. The poetry begins with a title: *Dragonfly with Red Wing-Tips in Pursuit of a Snake Sliding in a Spiral Towards the Comet Star*. In 1957 he began to work on the creation of *Walls of the Sun and the Moon* for the UNESCO building in Paris, for which he received the grand prix from the Guggenheim Foundation in 1959.

The opening of the Maeght Foundation took place in France in Saint Paul in 1964. One of the rooms in the museum and a garden called "Labyrinth" were given over to Joan Miró's art. Later, new sculptural compositions appeared in this garden which turned into Miró's amazing fairy-tale preserve.

In the 1960s he devoted enormous decorative panels to his favourite colour, light-blue. In each of them, against a light-blue background, only a few red or black spots and one delicate line, constitute both the space and balance of the composition, and the harmony of its colour (*Blue I*; *Blue III*). He received the highest awards in international exhibitions. However, his fascination always remained connected to the fairy tale, intimate world, delightful and mysterious. The artist, who suffered from heart failure, died in his home on December 25.

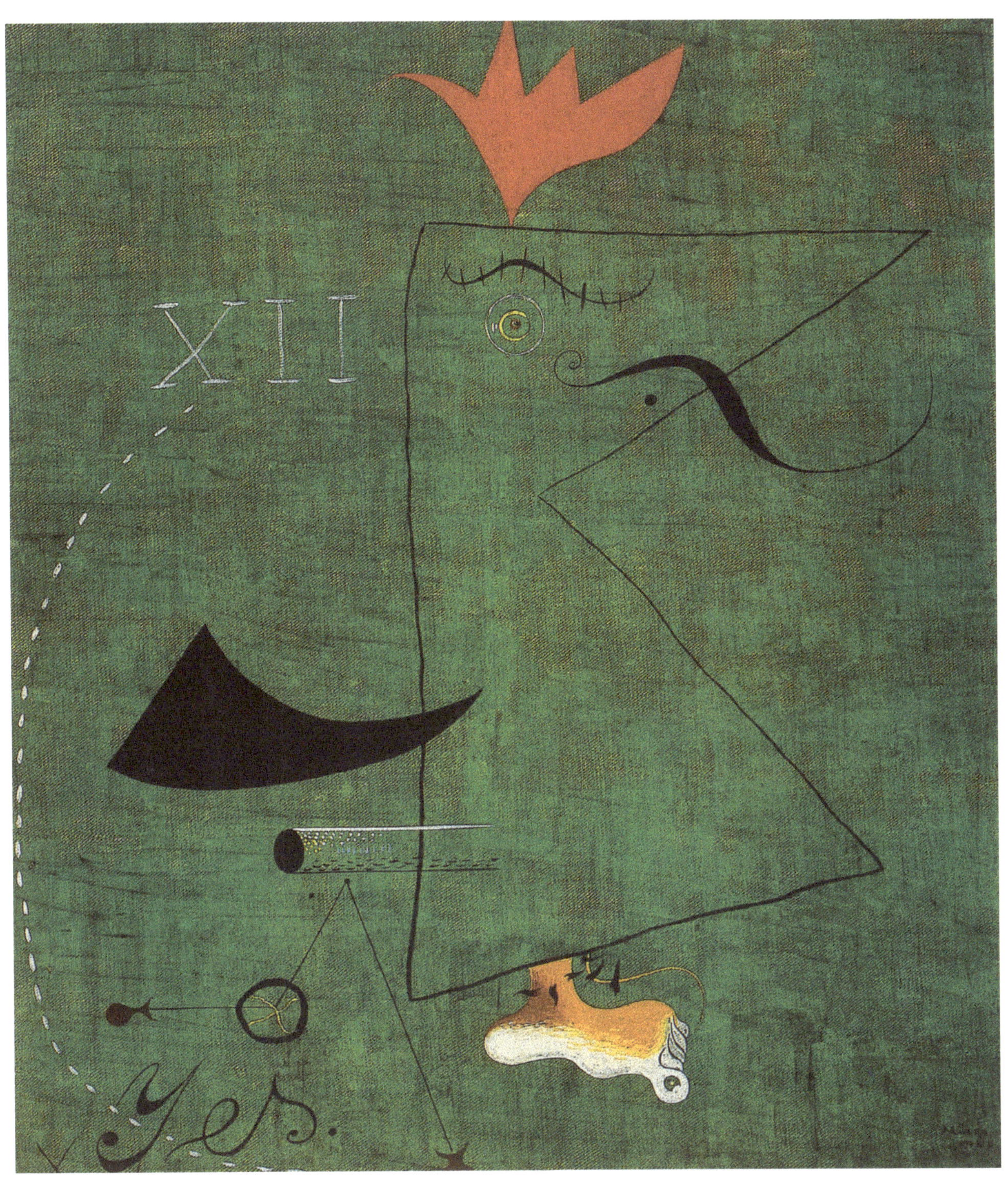

XII
Yes.

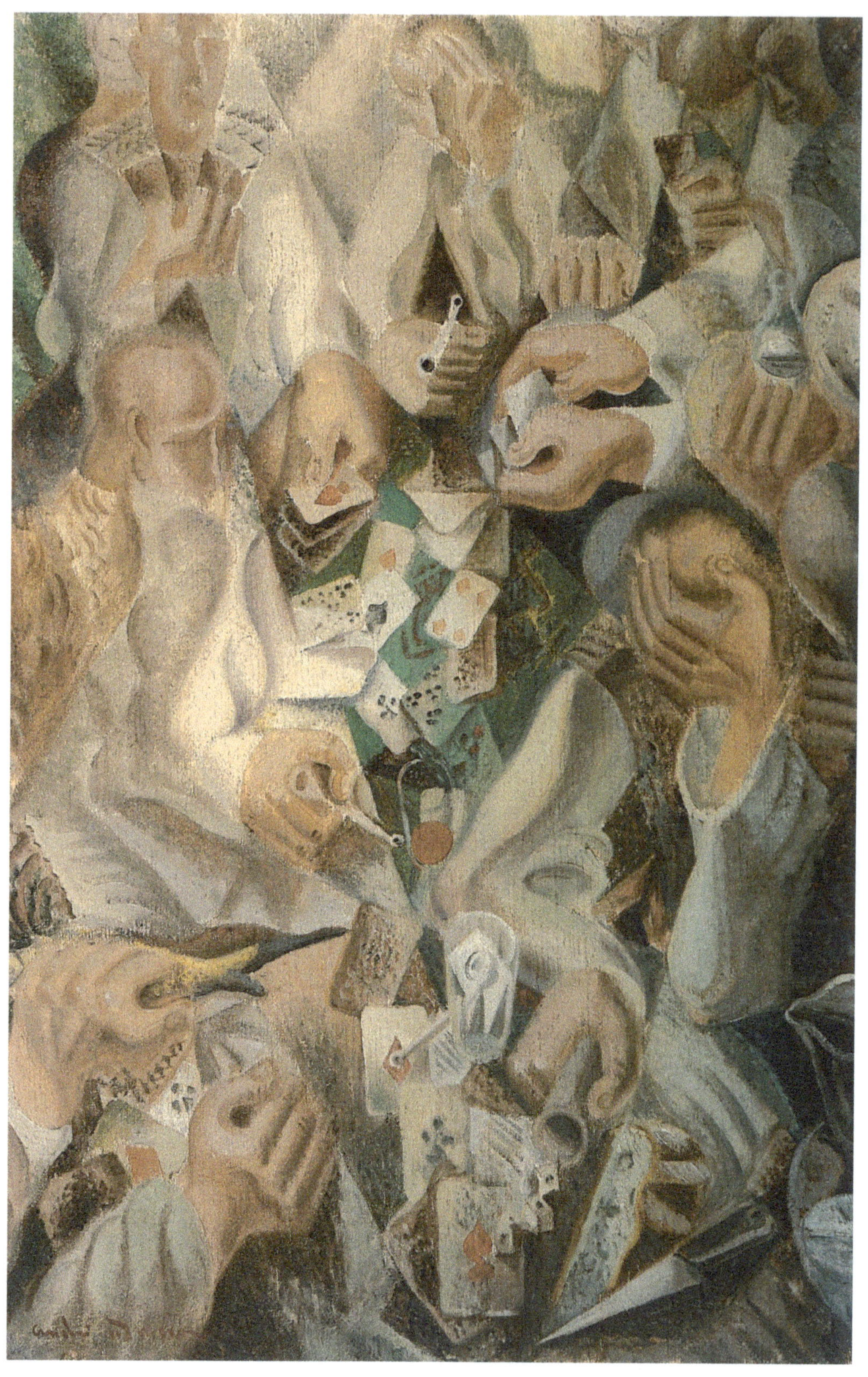

ANDRÉ MASSON

(Balagny-sur-Thérain 1896- Paris 1987)

t is impossible to separate the work of André Masson from Surrealism, despite the fact that he did not stay long within the membership of the group. In 1923, he associated himself with Breton, and in 1929 moved away from him and was excluded from the group. Breton's indignation did not upset Masson. He recognised that the leader of Surrealism was charismatic and persuasive.

André Masson was born to a peasant family in 1896 in the village of Baligny (Oise) in the Île-de-France. When he was eight, the family moved to Lille. It was there, in the museum, that Masson had his first glimpse of painting. When the family settled in Brussels, André began to learn drawing – in the morning and in the evening he studied at the Académie des Beaux-Arts. In Brussels, he saw a James Ensor exhibition.

Perhaps it was there that the interest in the strange and mysterious that would later lead him

◀ **André Masson,**
The Gamblers, 1923.
Oil on canvas, 81 x 54 cm.
Galerie Louise Leiris, Paris.

to Surrealism was awakened in him. One of André Masson's teachers was Constant Montald who introduced the young artist to the great Belgian poet Emilie Verhaeren. He persuaded Masson's parents to send André to study in Paris. In 1912, Masson was admitted to the École Nationale Supérieure des Beaux-Arts to study the technique of fresco painting.

In 1914, he succeeded in obtaining a government scholarship to travel to Italy and he went out to Tuscany to study fresco painting. For Masson, the war turned out to be a dreadful ordeal. At the age of twenty-one he was seriously wounded in the chest during the offensive at the Chemin des Dames. There followed long months spent in various hospitals, and it was only in 1919 at the age of twenty-three that he was able to resume a normal life.

In 1919, Masson settled in the little town of Caret near the Spanish border. Masson did not return to Paris until 1922. Contact with Kahnweiler in Paris not only enabled Masson to sell some of his works, but also brought him into a circle of artists. He got to know Derain and Juan Gris. As was bound to happen, one fine day André Breton turned up on the Rue Blomet as well, and he immediately bought the picture entitled *The Four Elements*, which Masson had just finished.

In Ceret, Masson painted landscapes in which admiration for the painting of Cézanne was palpable (*The Capuchin Convent at Ceret*). In 1923, in Paris, he painted still lifes in which traces of the Cubism of Juan Gris are evident (*Still Life with Candle*; *Card Trick*). In that same year, Masson's individual exhibition was held at the Galerie Simon. *The Four Elements* is the first enigmatic, symbolic picture in Masson's body of work. In 1925, he contributed to the first exhibition of Surrealist painting at the Galerie Pierre. André Breton's method captivated Masson.

Apparently the war had never ended for him. In order to convey his sense of the horror of slaughter and the nightmare of aggression, a conviction which from the time of the war had never left him, André Masson employed motifs from the life of animals. Starting from 1927, they predominate in his painting and drawings – as is obvious from their titles: *The Dead Horses*, *Horses Devouring Birds*, *Bird Shot by Arrows*, *The Trap and the Bird*.

In 1929, Breton excluded André Masson from the Surrealists, yet this did not have any impact on his art. His contemporaries continued to regard him as a Surrealist. The 1930s were the heyday both of Surrealism and Masson's creativity. His works took many different forms. He travelled to England in 1930. In 1932, he went to live near Grasse which meant that he was often able to spend time with Matisse. In 1934, he went to Spain for the first

time. This country made such an impression on them that they decided to leave France.

Masson settled in Catalonia. However, even in this beautiful country Masson discovered motifs connected to conflict and aggression, seeing them in the bullfight and in Spanish legends (*Massacre in a Field*). The defeat of the Republic in Spain compelled Masson, a committed supporter of the Republic, to return to France. Increasingly, the themes of ancient mythology – Pygmalion, the Labyrinth and the Minotaur – appeared in his painting.

In the 1930s, Masson began to work for the theatre, an occupation which assumed an important position in his life. He started in 1933 with the ballet, *Les Présages*, for the Russian ballet of Monte Carlo. In 1937. He made scenery and costumes for Barrault's theatre, for Cervantes's *Numance*, and for the drama *Hunger* by Knut Hamsun. Then there was Armand Salacrou's play, *The World is Round*, put on by Charles Dullin. Finally, in 1940 *Medea*, the opera by Darius Milhaud, was performed at the Paris Opera with Masson's scenery and costumes.

In 1939 and 1940, he completed portraits of the German Romantics, including several of Goethe (*Goethe and the Metamorphoses of Plants*). Masson continued to use sand in his painting; he gathered marine objects and fragments on the beaches of

André Masson, ▶
Armour, 1925.
Oil on canvas, 80.6 x 54 cm.
Peggy Guggenheim Collection, Venice.

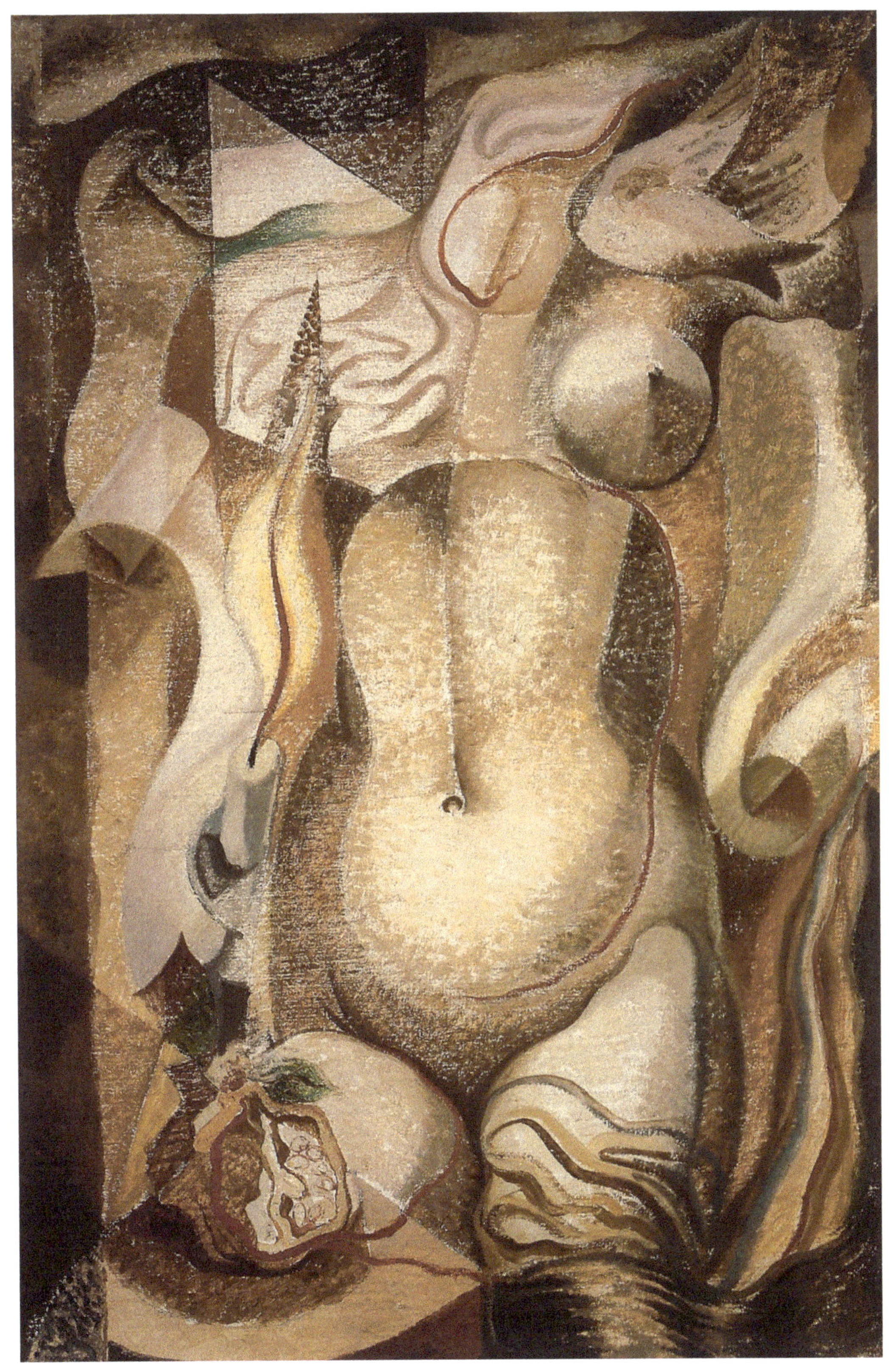

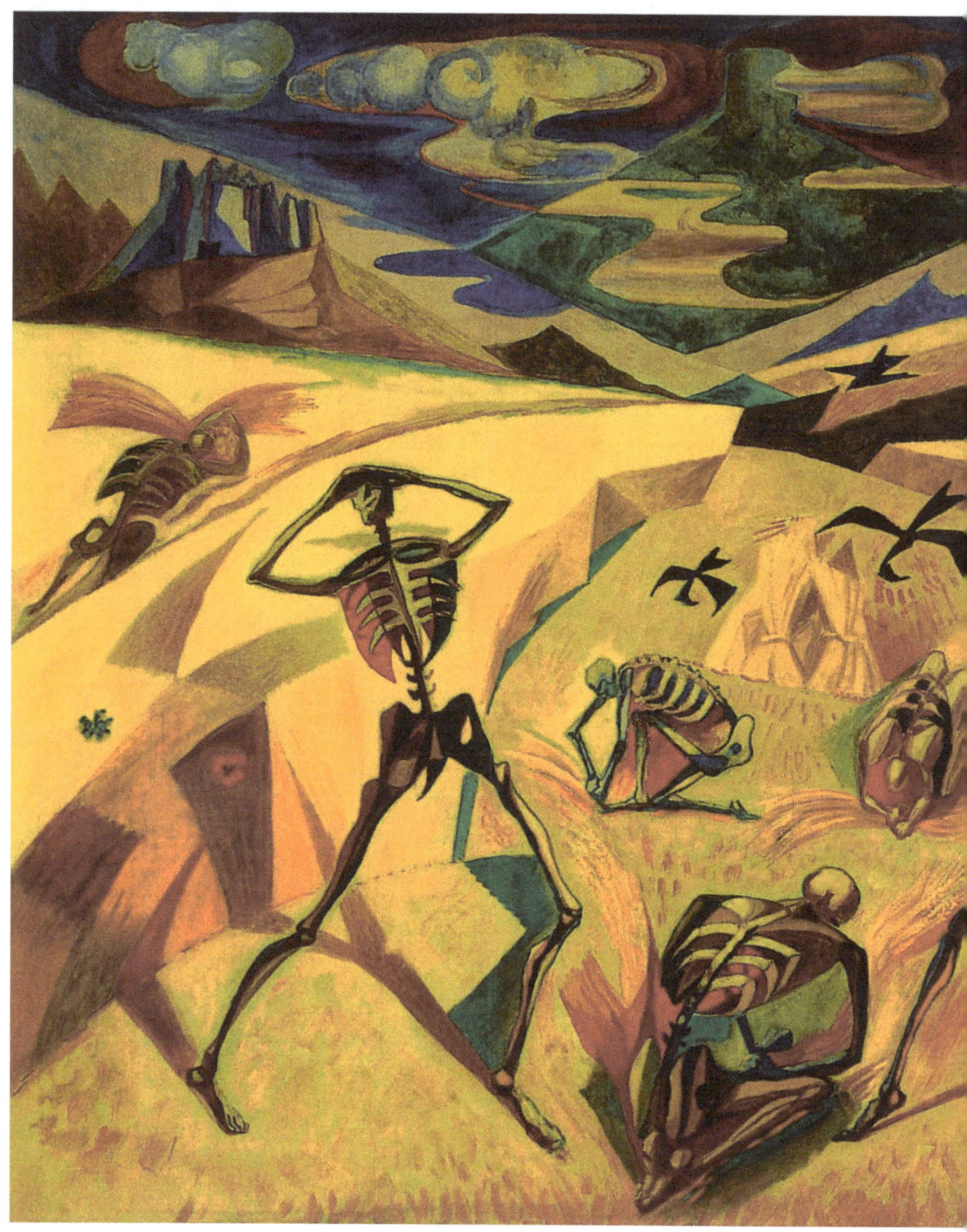

Brittany, and he used them in his pictures as well. The war, however, brought this life to an abrupt end.

In 1940, settled in Connecticut, where they met Yves Tanguy. Masson worked together with Breton and took an active part in the Surrealists' events and exhibitions in America. In October 1945, as soon as it was possible, Masson and his family returned to France.

In Paris, Masson immediately resumed work for the theatre of Jean-Louis Barrault: he made scenery and costumes for *Hamlet* and for Jean-Paul Sartre's play *Men Without Shadows*. In 1947 he returned to Aix-en-Provence where he lived in the same locality where Paul Cézanne painted Mont Saint-Victoire. The south of France fascinated Masson. He painted the landscapes of Provence and pictures that were inspired by them. Masson was known all over the world by now and behind Masson's work stood a man who was unusual, remarkable, and in his way enigmatic.

In 1965 he painted the ceiling of the Odéon-Theâtre de France. Masson also was a talented author, and wrote two books of memoirs: *Vagabond of Surrealism* and *Rebel of Surrealism* – throughout his life he regarded himself as a Surrealist. André Masson died in Paris on 28 October 1987 at the age of ninety-one.

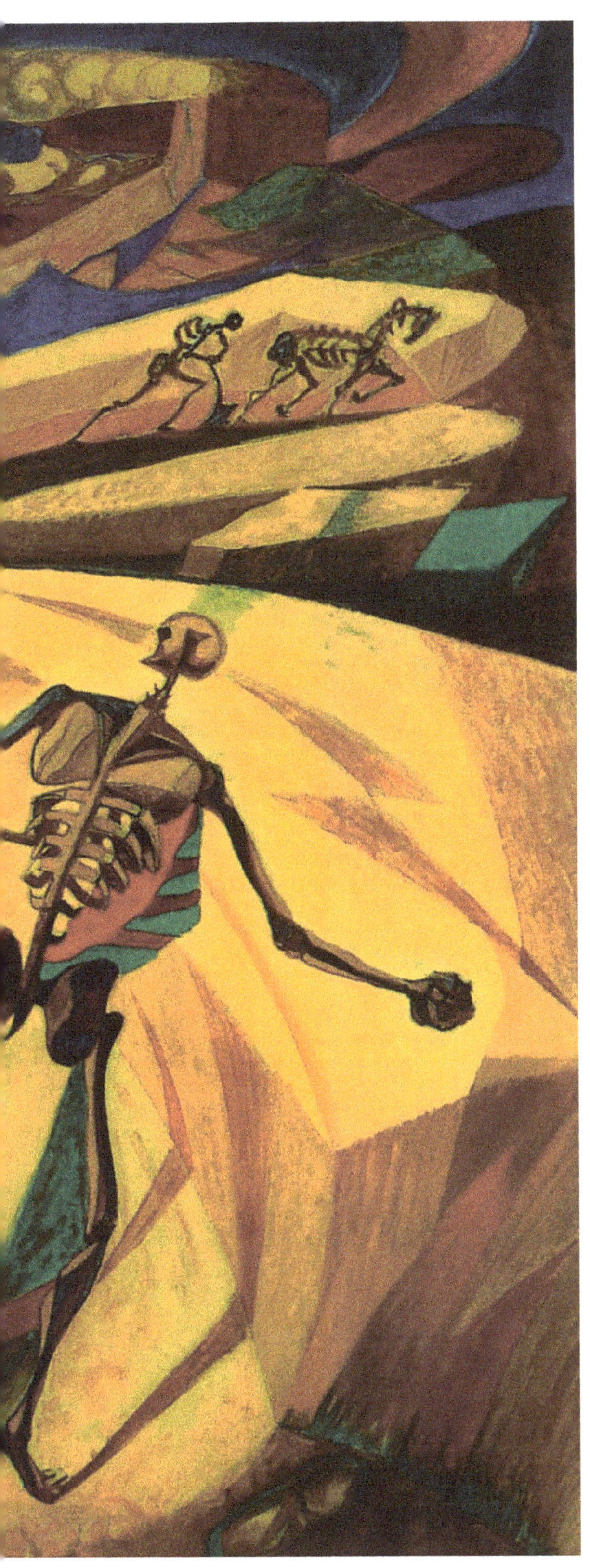

◀ **André Masson**,
The Andalusian Harvest Workers, 1935.
Oil on canvas, 89 x 116 cm.
Galerie Louise Leiris, Paris.

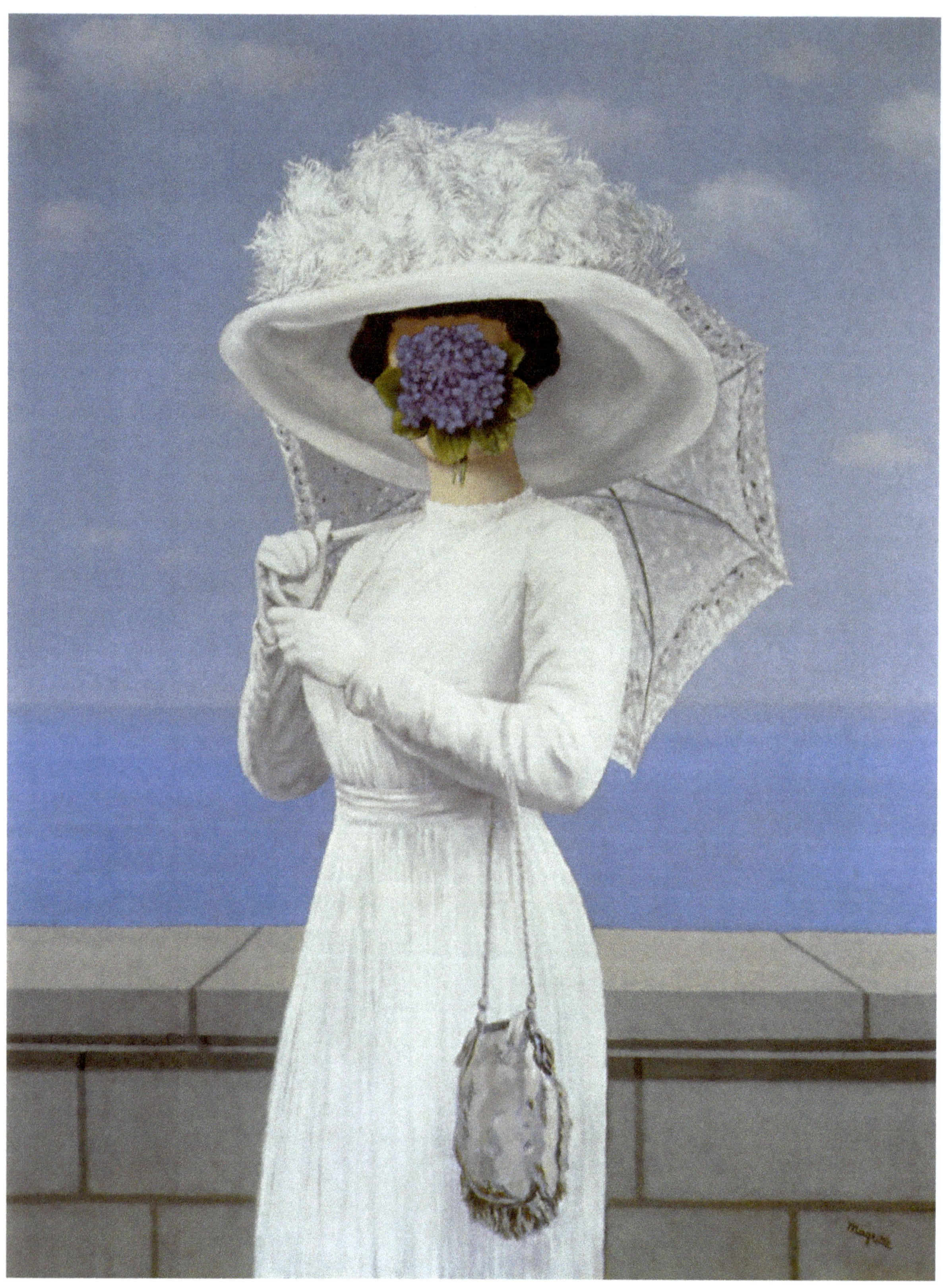

RENÉ MAGRITTE

(Lessines 1898- Brussels 1967)

René Magritte was born in Lessines, Belgium, on 21 November 1898. His father was a merchant and his mother a milliner. When René was six or seven years old, he stayed with his aunts in Soignies during school holidays. There, in the local cemetery, his first encounter with an artist took place. In his imagination, it forever linked painting with the world of the strange and mysterious.

René Magritte began to draw at the age of twelve. When he was fourteen, his mother committed suicide one night by throwing herself into the Sambre River. When he was fifteen, on the merry-go-round at a local fair, René met a girl by the name of Georgette Berger who later became his wife. His first work in painting, in the spirit of Impressionism, dates from 1915. The following year, he enrolled as a student at the Académie des Beaux-Arts in Brussels.

In the Belgian capital, Magritte came into contact with the milieu that would have a decisive role in his artistic formation. Magritte rented a studio together with Pierre-Louis Flouquet, and he made friends with the poet Pierre Bourgeois. The three of them began to publish the journal *Au volant!* At this time, Magritte painted pictures that are reminiscent of Picasso's early Cubism, and he exhibited one of them, called *Three Women*.

After World War I, the cultural life in Brussels was becoming more active. In Brussels, new galleries sprang up which were interested in Modernist tendencies in art. In 1923, Paul Nouge, Marcel Lecomte and Camille Goemans founded the journal *Correspondance*, and René Magritte, Edouard Mesens, and several others joined them. This was the beginning of Surrealism in Belgium.

Magritte's Surrealism sprang from the same source as the Surrealism of Yves Tanguy. The artist himself told the story of how, in 1922, Marcel Lecomte showed him a reproduction of Giorgio de Chirico's painting, *The Song of Love*, and how he could not hold backs the tears.

However, it is possible that the truly prophetic painting which points towards Magritte's future Surrealist path, is something he created in 1926,

◀ **René Magritte**,
The Great War, 1964.
Oil on canvas, 81 x 60 cm.
Private Collection, Washington, D. C.

The Man from the Sea. Here, many influences are apparent: memories of Fantômas, of the constructions from drawing instruments in de Chirico's paintings, of Hans Arp's abstract figures. Nevertheless, the design of the painting stands apart, and is absolutely independent of any influences.

In the course of 1925 and 1926, Magritte painted more than sixty canvases, made a great number of collages, and worked in the advertising field. In the spring of 1927, two galleries, Le Centaure and P.G. van Hecke, signed contracts with him which allowed the artist to devote himself exclusively to painting. At this time, he decided to move to France, and in 1927 René and Georgette Magritte settled in Paris. Magritte, as was natural, joined the group of Paris Surrealists on equal terms with the other members. However, in 1930 Magritte cut his ties with Breton and returned to Brussels. He did not like to talk about himself, and gave no one an explanation for the break.

One of the key devices in Magritte's paintings is the pipe, the first example of which he painted in 1929, with the inscription, "This is not a pipe". In this picture, Magritte yoked representation and speech together in a single composition, and this became one of the main themes of his painting. Words became an inseparable element of his painting. In one instance, he accompanies words on the canvas with dots in the manner of a map in an atlas: tree, cloud, village on the horizon, etc., and calls the picture *Swift Hope*. In another instance, the words themselves become representative objects, and he writes them at points he has set aside on his canvas: a figure bursting out laughing, horizon, wardrobe, cried of birds; and calls

it *The Living Mirror*. Moreover, each word is written in his vivid handwriting, and in this way becomes a graphic element of the picture.

The title of a Magritte painting is another of his enigmas and another of the ideas behind his painting. If the words "This is not a pipe" can be treated as an explanation of the fact that the representation of the object is not the object itself, then the title of the picture does more to conceal its sense than to reveal it: *The Treachery of Images*.

The artist's play space and the strange transformations of interiors and landscapes remained one of his obsessions in the 1930s. A window is smashed, and splinters of glass on which fragments of the landscape have left their imprint are scattered on all sides (*The Key to the Fields*). The image of an eagle turned to stone was to remain a constant feature of his work. It is real, and other birds flock towards it, but the cracked stone of which it consists is also real (*Lost Steps*).

For a short period, Magritte changed his painting technique. His technique became like that of the Impressionists, but his images were still the old, enigmatic images of Magritte: a mermaid with the face of Georgette dozes on a pink sofa (*The Forbidden Universe*); living toes grow out of a pair of boots standing beside a wooden wall (*The Red Model*).

René Magritte, ▶
The Castle in the Pyrenees, 1959.
Oil on canvas, 200 x 145 cm.
The Israel Museum, Jerusalem.

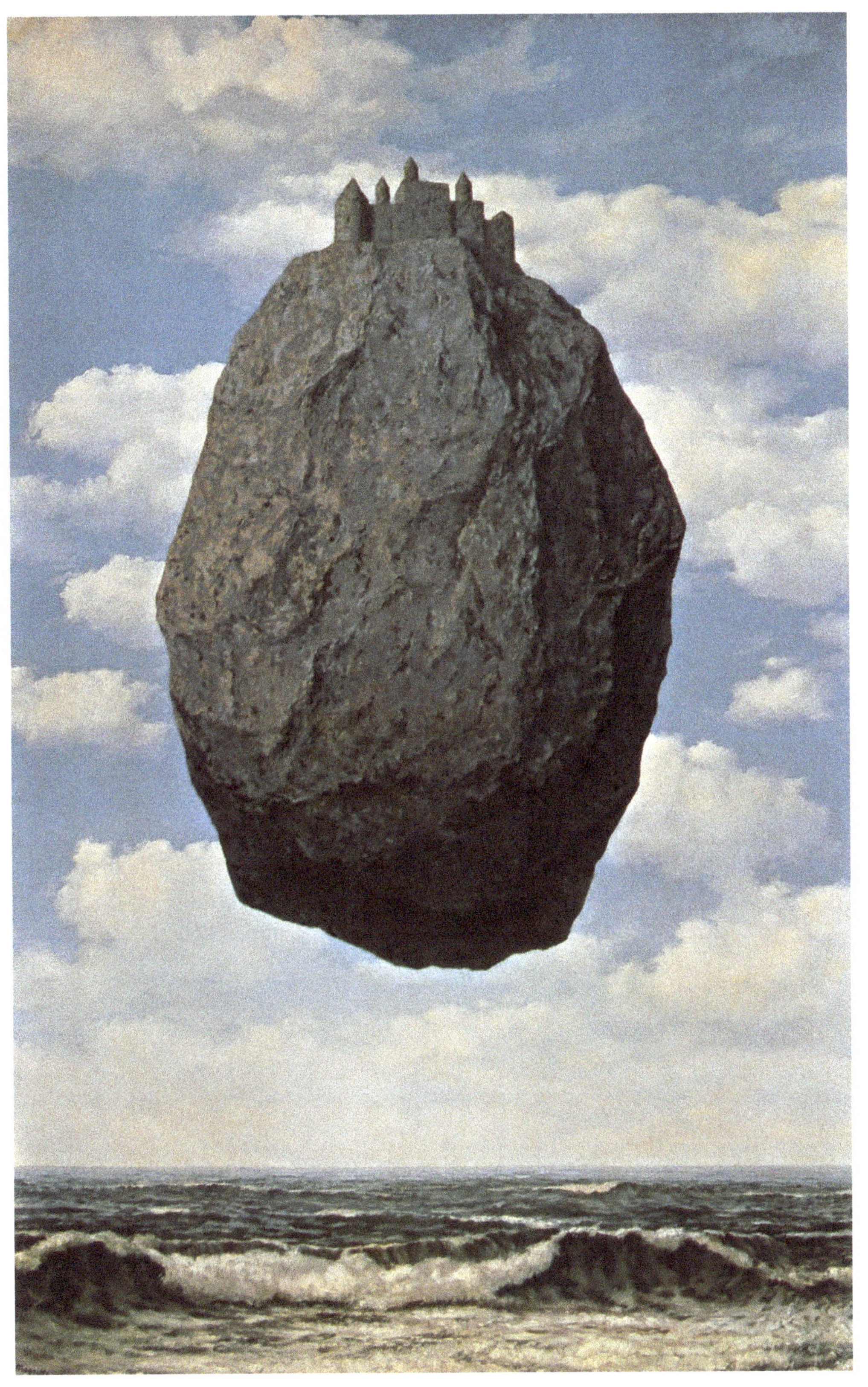

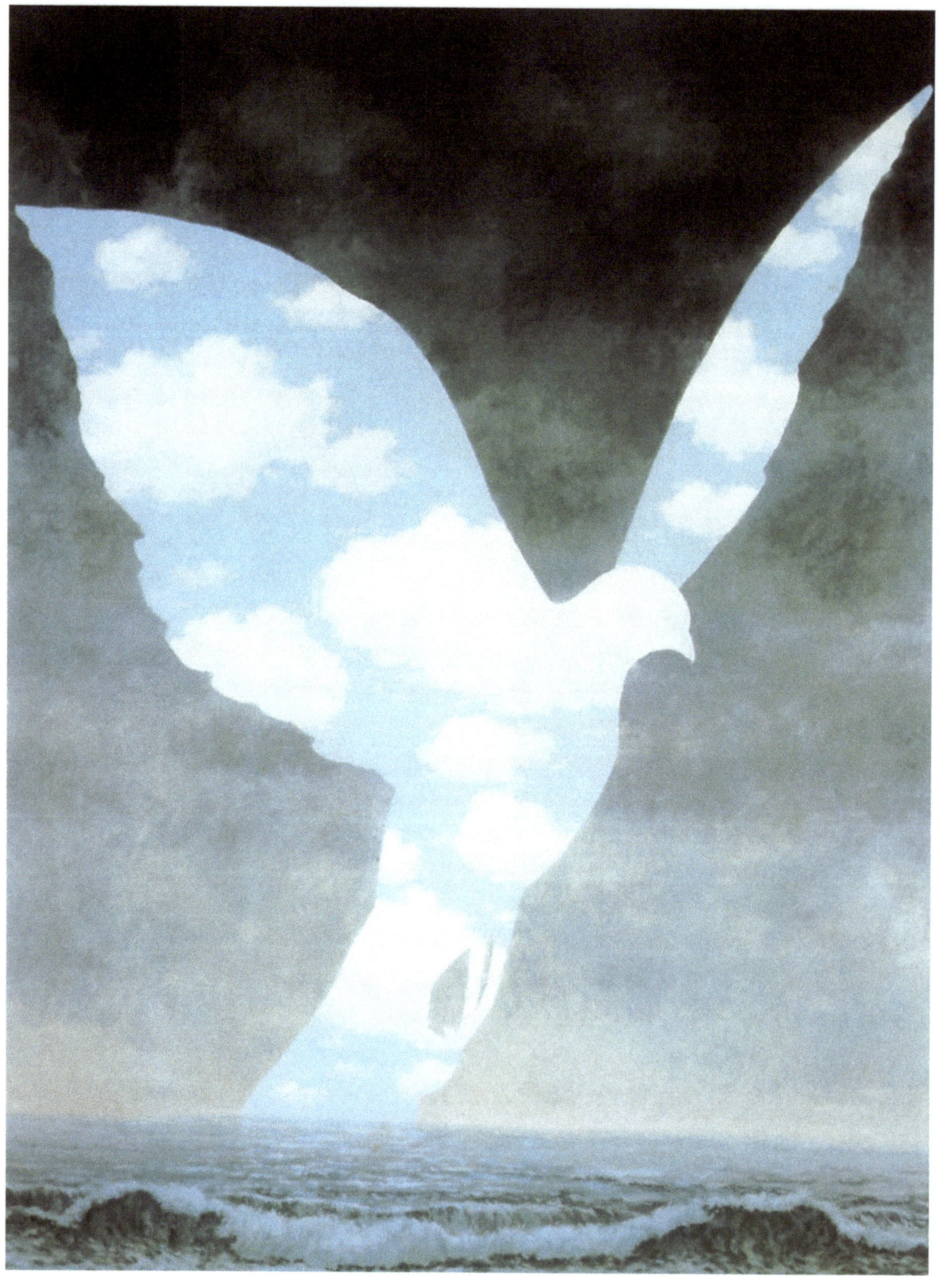

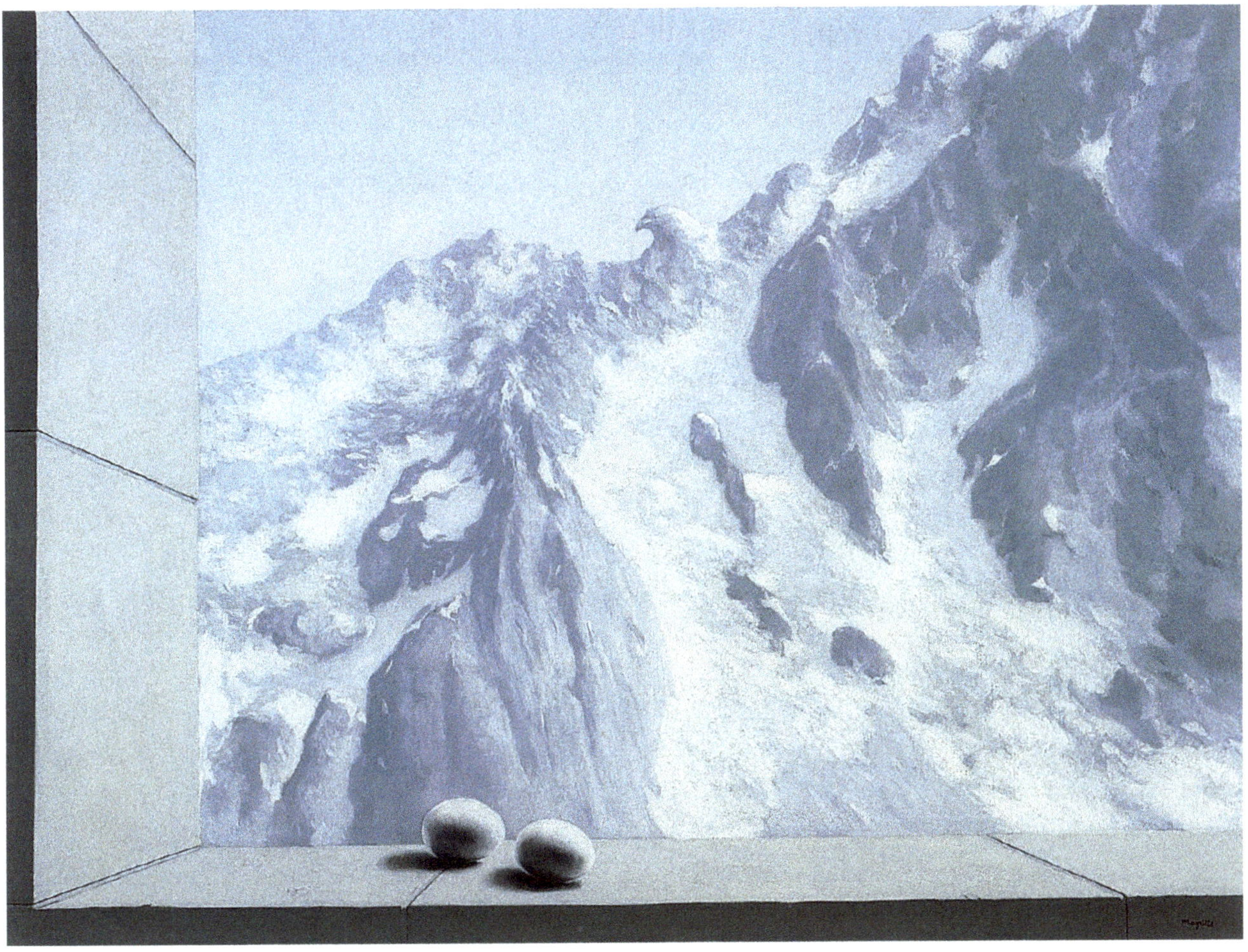

◀ **René Magritte**,
The Big Family, 1963.
Oil on canvas, 100 x 81 cm.
Utsunomiya Museum of Art, Utsunomiya.

René Magritte, ▲
The Domain of Arnheim, 1938.
Oil on canvas, 73 x 100 cm.
Private Collection.

One of the most interesting of the series he completed was that on the theme of *Memory of a Journey*. Magritte depicted his friend, the poet Marcel Lecomte, in the prosaic setting of a room, standing in an overcoat with a book in his hand (*Travel Memory III*). The only unusual detail is the lion lying in the room. In the monumental canvas, *The Castle in the Pyrenees*, a whole rock is suspended over an expanse of the sea, and the castle sits on top of the rock. This is a frightening scene, yet in the reality of the painting, there is nothing frightening about it. It is instead a poetic image of a castle from a dream, "between heaven and earth".

Belgium recognised René Magritte as one of its greatest artists. He died on 15 August 1967 at his home in Belgium.

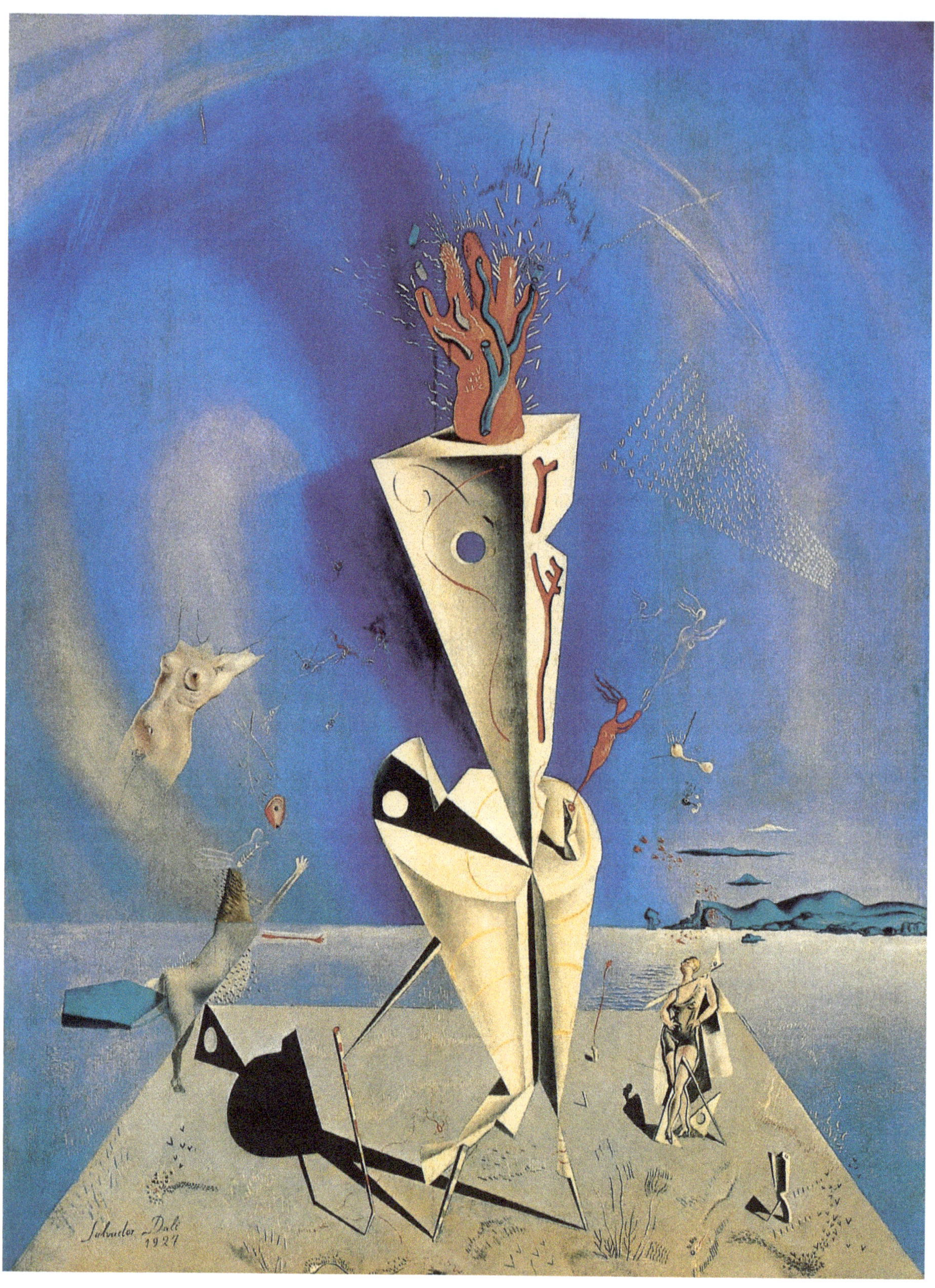

SALVADOR DALÍ

(1904 - Figueras 1989)

Salvador Dalí loved "the eternal Catalonia" and his wife Gala, Elena Diakonova. But what he loved most of all was himself and his work. He spent his life shaping the image of his genius, assembling it from the very smallest elements like a childish builder with his fragile model of little bricks. He lovingly sharpened and polished it, adding on more and more new details.

Salvador Dalí was born on 11 May 1904, in the town of Figueres in Catalonia. His father, Salvador Dalí y Cusi, was a notary in Figueres. Brought up in his sister's anti-clerical family, he sent his son to the local school. When Salvador reached the age of eight, his father moved him to the École Catholique de la Salle. At this school, Dalí learned to speak French like a native. It was here that he received his first lessons in painting and drawing.

His father allowed Salvador to set up his studio in the attic. Mother, grandmother and aunt immensely

◀ **Salvador Dalí,**
Apparatus and Hand, 1927.
Oil on wood, 62.2 x 47.6 cm.
The Salvador Dalí Museum, ancient E. and A. Reynolds Morse Collection, Saint Petersburg (Florida, USA).

spoiled the sickly little boy. Later on, he completed a portrait of himself at that age at Cadaques – a little boy with very big eyes and a scarf at his throat, sitting with the sea in the background, a bottle of medicine on the table, and a little parrot in a cage (*The Sick Child: Self-Portrait at Cadaques*).

In 1921, his mother, Felipa Domenech, died. For Salvador, who had admired her, this was a cruel blow. Very soon afterwards, his father married his wife's sister, Catalina. In his books, Salvador Dalí paid much attention to childhood impressions. It turns out that Dalí had an elder brother who died of meningitis seven years before he was born. Dalí never saw his brother, but he was given the same name – Salvador, Saviour – and all his life Dalí had the sense of a certain duality, as though he lived in a state of coexistence with his brother and inhabited the same being. At the end of his life Salvador Dalí continued to paint portraits of the first Salvador, his brother (*Portrait of my Deceased Brother*).

In 1917, at the age of thirteen years, he received the artistic Academy's diploma and first prize for the best drawing. In 1914, he painted a portrait of his nurse, Lucia (*Portrait of Lucia*). The old woman's face is painted with uncompromising expressiveness. Dalí's painting from around this time attests to the fact that he was then already thinking not only about colour, but also about the role that a vivid surface could play in the expressiveness of the work. A self-portrait by the sixteen-year-old Dalí shows him as a handsome, refined youth with a meditative expression in his large eyes and the proud countenance of Don Quixote (*Self-Portrait with Raphael's Neck*).

In the summer of 1928, Dalí invited Luis Buñuel, his other friend from the period of his university residence life, to Figueres and Cadaques. Buñuel had been in Paris in 1925, where he had met the Surrealists. While still in Madrid, Buñuel and Dalí planned to make a Surrealist film. Both of them got down to work on it at Cadaques. In his memoirs, Dalí said that he did not like Buñuel's scenario, and that he rewrote it.

Their most effective discovery was the close-up of the film in which a razor-blade cuts into a living human eye. Dalí was very pleased with how they had managed to get the revolting shot of the dead donkeys, on which he had poured glue, afterwards enlarging their jaws so as to make a frightening grin. On 6 June 1929, the silent film *Un Chien andalou* was shown in Paris. Dalí came to Paris for its screening. He wanted the mixture of eroticism, death, and disgust with which he had filled the seventeen minutes of his film to shock and to amaze the viewers. The opinions of the press were divided: the horror of some publications counterbalanced the excitement of those others who were on the side of Surrealism.

Rumours about the talented Catalan had already reached the Paris Surrealists. Dalí was in Paris for the first time in 1924. One of the Spanish artists introduced him to Picasso. Picasso invited Dalí to his studio. It appears as though the artists were appraising each other's work. There was already one Catalan in the Surrealist group – Joan Miró. Now Miró introduced Dalí to the Surrealists.

In Dalí's private life, 1929 was marked by two events. First, he showed one of his pictures in an exhibition in Paris alongside some words insulting to the memory of his mother, and this was to cause Dalí's rupture with his family. The artist's father forbade him to return home to Figueres. Second, during his stay in Paris Dalí invited the Surrealist group to come and stay with him in Cadaques. That summer, along with Buñuel, the art dealer Camille Goemans and his wife came to stay with him, as well as René Magritte and his wife, and Paul Éluard and his wife.

A love affair between Salvador and Gala Éluard flared up at once, with dramatic consequences. Dalí describes his trepidation and indecisiveness at Cadaques in some detail, as well as the way Gala responded to his feelings. He writes that she cured him of the state of madness in which he then found himself. He called her by the name of Gradiva – a girl from the novel of the writer V. Jensen who cures the hero of his spiritual sickness. The Surrealists' muse became, from that moment, Dalí's personal muse. Éluard carried on hoping for

Salvador Dalí, ▶
Portrait of Paul Éluard, 1929.
Oil on cardboard, 33 x 25 cm.
Private Collection.

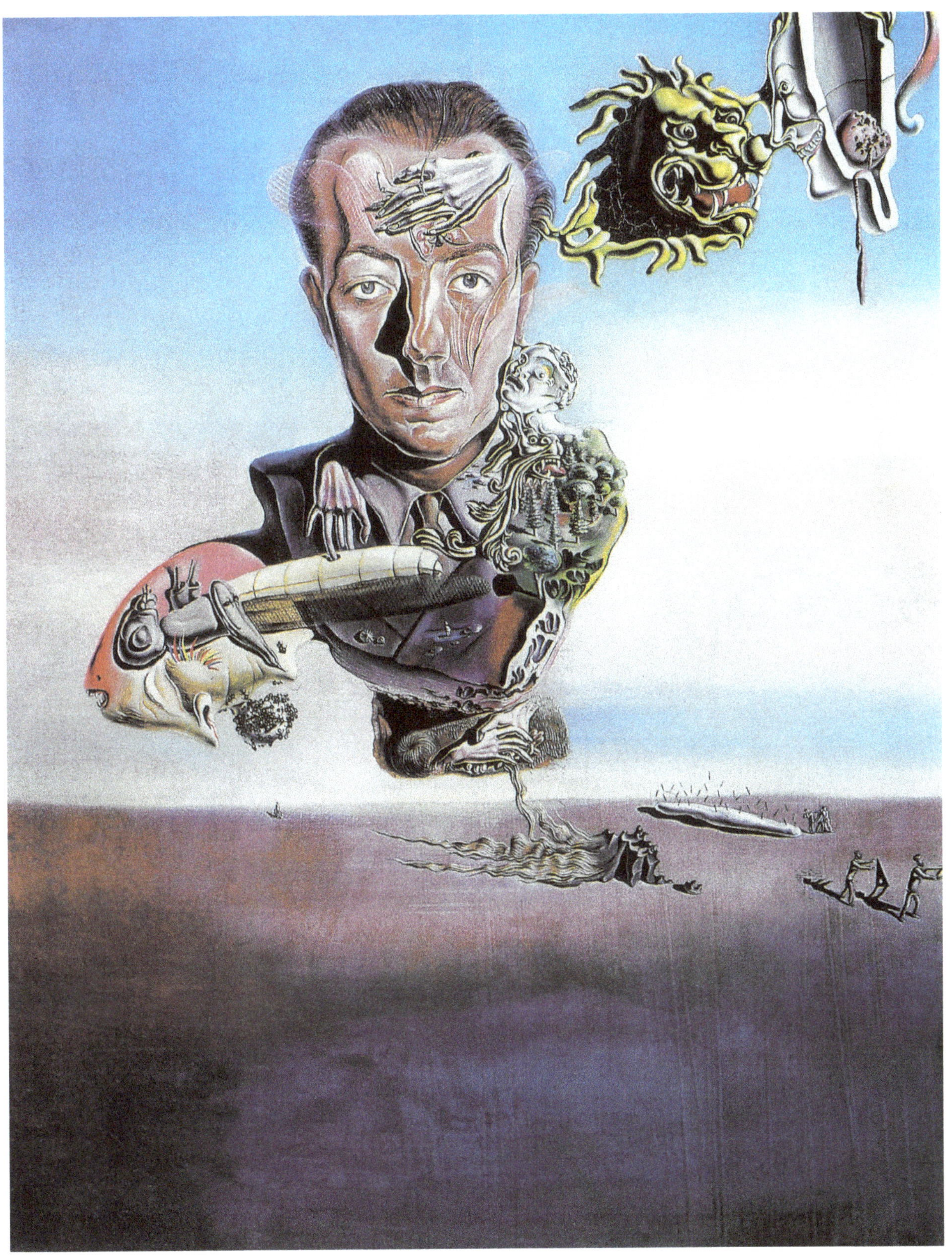

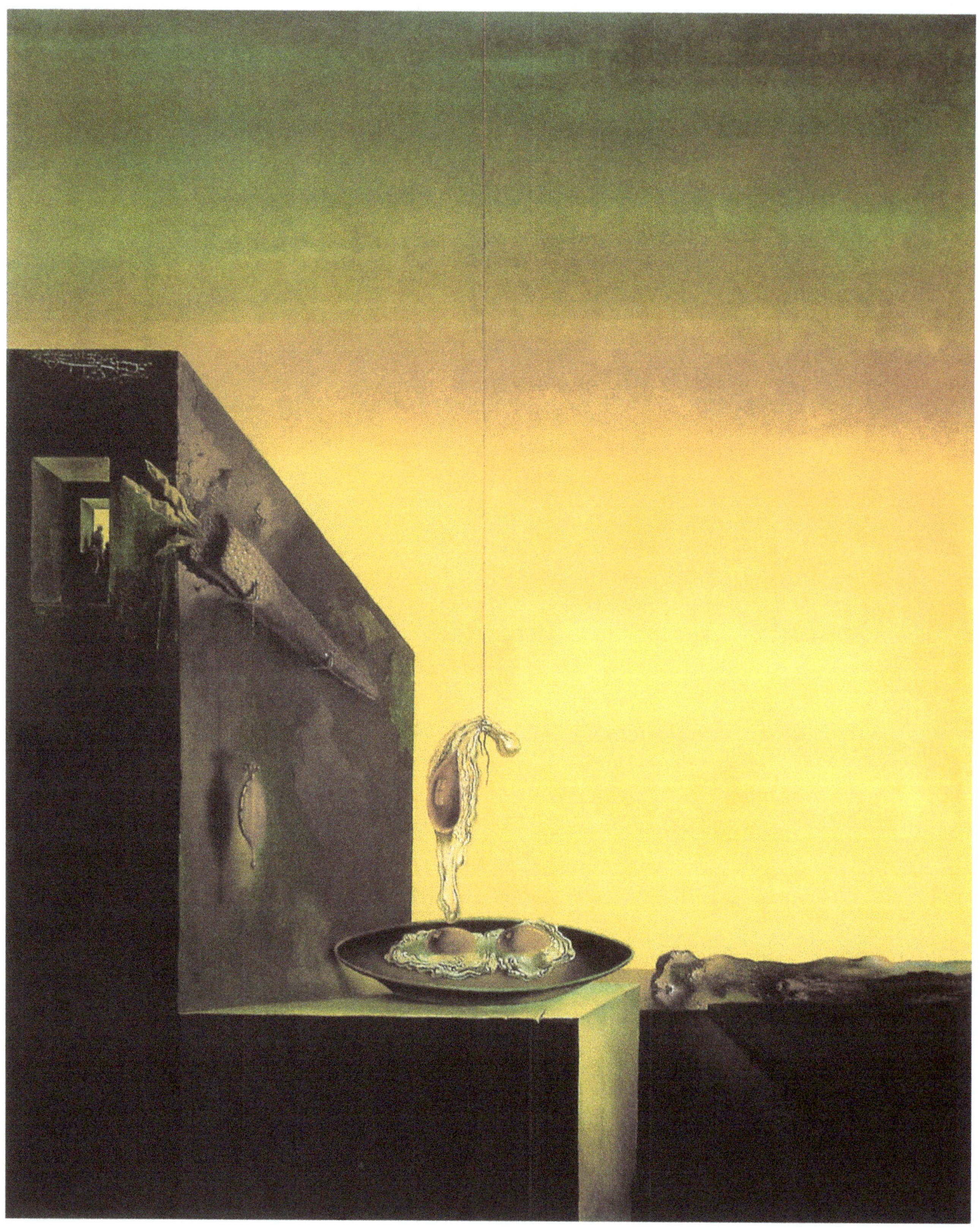

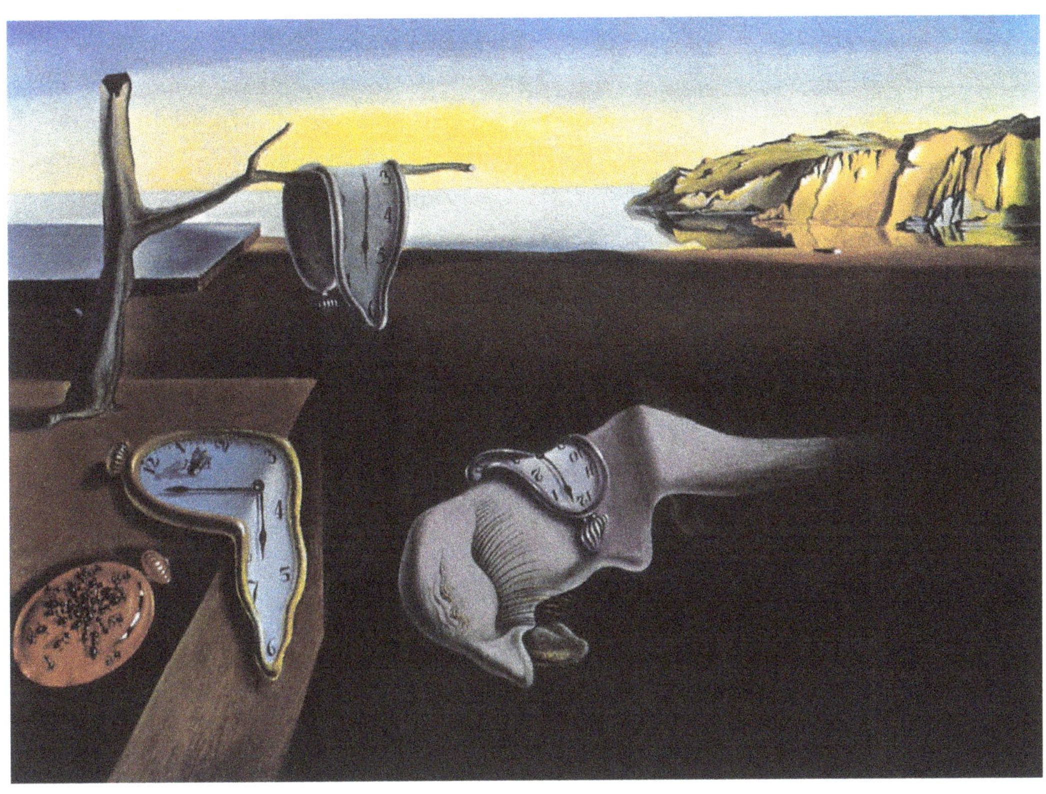

Gala's return for a long time. But in the summer of 1929, everything was finally decided. To the end of her life Gala would remain the wife, sister, secretary, assistant, and chief advisor to Salvador Dalí. Each of his works was marked by his worship of Gala. Throughout the whole of his work, Dalí painted and drew new pictures of Gala again and again.

For him, Gala was the Madonna (*The Madonna of Port Lligat*). She was his Leda (*Leda Atomica*). Even in those instances where the picture bore an entirely Surrealist character, Gala remained as beautiful a woman as the artist's classical skill could make her (*Portrait of Gala with Two Lamb Chops Balanced on Her Shoulder; Paranoiac Metamorphosis of Gala's Face; Portrait of Gala with Symptoms of Rhinoceritis*). Dalí came into contact with the Surrealists at the age of twenty-five. By this time he was already a Surrealist himself. The film, *Un Chien Andalou*, serves as evidence of this.

As regards Surrealism, as it took shape in the works of Dalí, a large influence turns out to have been his familiarity with the painting of the Paris artists. He even directly borrowed certain elements that other Surrealists had already found. Sometimes the shadows in a Dalí picture openly acknowledge their debt to the painting of Giorgio de Chirico. And, of course, Dalí noticed the simple and brilliant inventions of René Magritte (*Tower of Pleasure,* or *Vertigo*).

Salvador Dalí took the lessons of Sigmund Freud much more seriously than any others. He said that Freud's ideas had the same significance for him as the Bible had had for the medieval masters. In his memoirs, Dalí relates almost all the images of his painting to childhood impressions. This is the case, even without acknowledging that none of the Surrealists applied the teaching of Freud on the libido as literally and with such obsessive consistency as did Dalí. One of his first truly Surrealist pictures was *The Great Masturbator.*

In 1931, Dalí painted *The Persistence of Memory.* He told the story of how the image of this picture came to him one evening when Gala went out with friends to the cinema and he stayed at home. By changing the usual properties of objects, Dalí found a means to provoke the feeling of disgust he so favoured and cultivated in the viewer of the painting. Following the watches, a violin was melted and hung up like a crumpled rag (*Masochistic Instrument*). Next, a grand piano was transformed into a piece of cloth so as to make it look as though one could pull it by the corner and remove it like a cover (*The Pharmacist Carefully Removing the Cover of a Grand Piano*). The Surrealist world of Salvador Dalí was transformed into a world of insane objects which had ceased to be what they should have been. Finally, the head of the artist himself was subjected to this kind of transformation and also lost its solidity, while still retaining the fine likeness of a portrait (*Soft Self-Portrait with Grilled Lard*).

At the beginning of the 1930s, Francois Millet's painting, *The Angelus,* became another of Dalí's obsessions. In several of Dalí's compositions, this picture appeared as a whole, and it was the only real object in its Surrealist setting (*Gala and the Angelus of Millet Preceding the Imminent Arrival of the Comical Anamorphoses*). The "Angelus" became Dalí's property, and he supplemented the composition by Millet with new details, and changed the figures' poses (*Retrospective Female Bust; Portrait of Gala or the Angelus of Gala*).

The metamorphosis of *Angelus* in his paintings was prompted by its dark poetry and mystery of death, especially after Dalí became conscious of the alteration in the picture that had been made by Millet himself: research has shown that a grave had at first been depicted between the female and the male figures (*Twilight Atavisms (Obsessive Phenomenon); Archeological Reminiscence of Millet's Angelus; The Architectonic Angelus of Millet*).

Dalí's idol was Vermeer of Delft. Vermeer, seated behind the easel or the town of Delft, appears in the Dalian landscape (*Enigmatic Elements in a Landscape; Apparition of the City of Delft*). The

Salvador Dalí, ▶
Mae West's Face which May Be Used as a Surrealist Appartment,
1934-1935.
Gouache, with graphite, on commercially printed
magazine page, 28.3 x 17.8 cm.
The Art Institute of Chicago, Chicago.

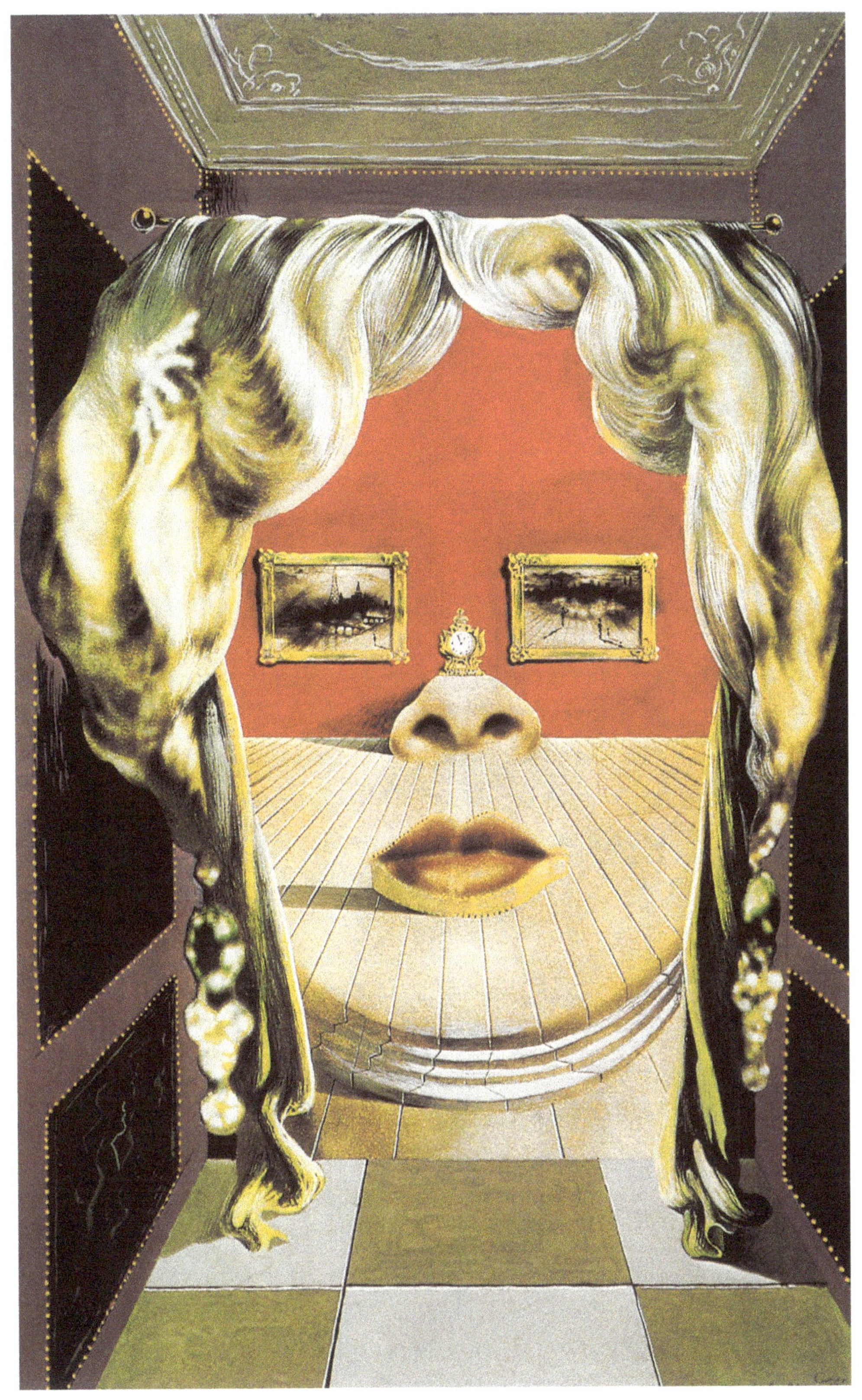

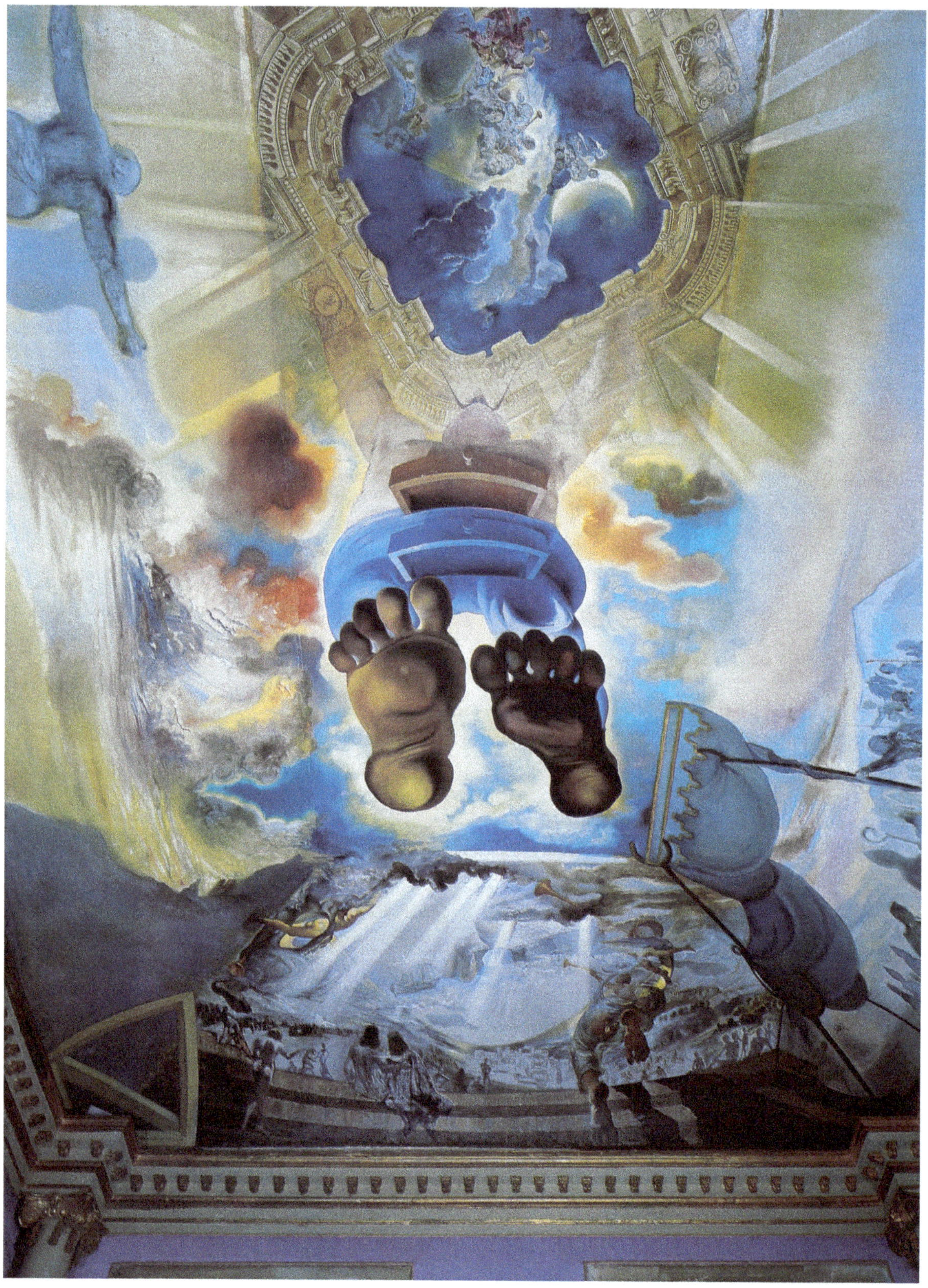

figures of Vermeer himself, or of his protagonists, are never rendered ugly or disgusting, and yet, as with all the objects in Dalí's world, they are subjected to transformation. The result of transformations like these was to become one of the most brilliant of Dalí's discoveries – his furniture figure.

Even the Venus de Milo underwent a "furniture" metamorphosis. The wooden drawers thrust themselves forward from living flesh, causing it pain (*The Anthropomorphic Cabinet*). The most vivid result of the development of paintings of this type is *Giraffes on Fire*. The paradox of the flaming giraffe in the background is itself a statement about the dreadful unnaturalness of what is happening in the painting.

In the words of Dalí himself, "the first poem and the first picture entirely obtained from the complete application of the paranoiac-critical method" was Narcissus (*Metamorphosis of Narcissus*). The transformation of Narcissus occurs under the viewer's eyes.

In July 1936, the Spanish Civil War began. Dalí repeatedly stated that he was an apolitical man. His picture, *The Enigma of Hitler*, cost him, in his own words, "anathemas from the Nazi side and stormy applause from the camp of their opponents". This picture gave rise to a serious conflict between Dalí and the Surrealists. However, Catalonia, and Spain

as a whole, were his great loves. And perhaps no politically oriented artist expressed his anguish over Spain with as much force as did Dalí (*The Automobile Fossil of Cap de Creus*).

In the course of the 1930s, Dalí's painting was shown more than once in the Surrealists' group exhibitions and in his own individual exhibitions, including those held in America. In 1934 and 1936, he spent time in the United States. With the beginning of World War II, many European artists went to North America. Dalí and Gala also headed there in 1939. He resumed his work in the cinema and he collaborated with Alfred Hitchcock and Walt Disney. However, from 1939 everything changed. Breton excluded Dalí from the Surrealist group. He called Dalí, cleverly changing the places of the letters in his name, "Avida Dollars" – the idea of bourgeois self-enrichment was alien to the Surrealists.

Dalí's paintings of Christian themes date from the post-war era, beginning with a Madonna, and ending with *The Last Supper*, and with various versions of the Crucifixion (*The Christ of Saint John of the Cross*). At the same time, he continued to make pictures from a series of visions, in which he endeavoured with scrupulous precision, to reproduce the images of dreams (*Dream Caused by the Flight of a Bee Around a Pomegranate a Second Before Waking up*. For the majority of people in the world who appreciated Surrealism, Dalí did indeed become the personification of it. In 1982, a terrible misfortune befell the artist – Gala died. At almost eighty years old, the artist immediately found himself helpless and lost; he fell seriously ill and he was robbed by his secretary. Dalí spent his last years chiefly in Spain, where he died in his castle in 1989.

◀ **Salvador Dalí**,
Palace of the Wind, 1972.
Painting of the ceiling of old Teatro Museo.
Figueres.

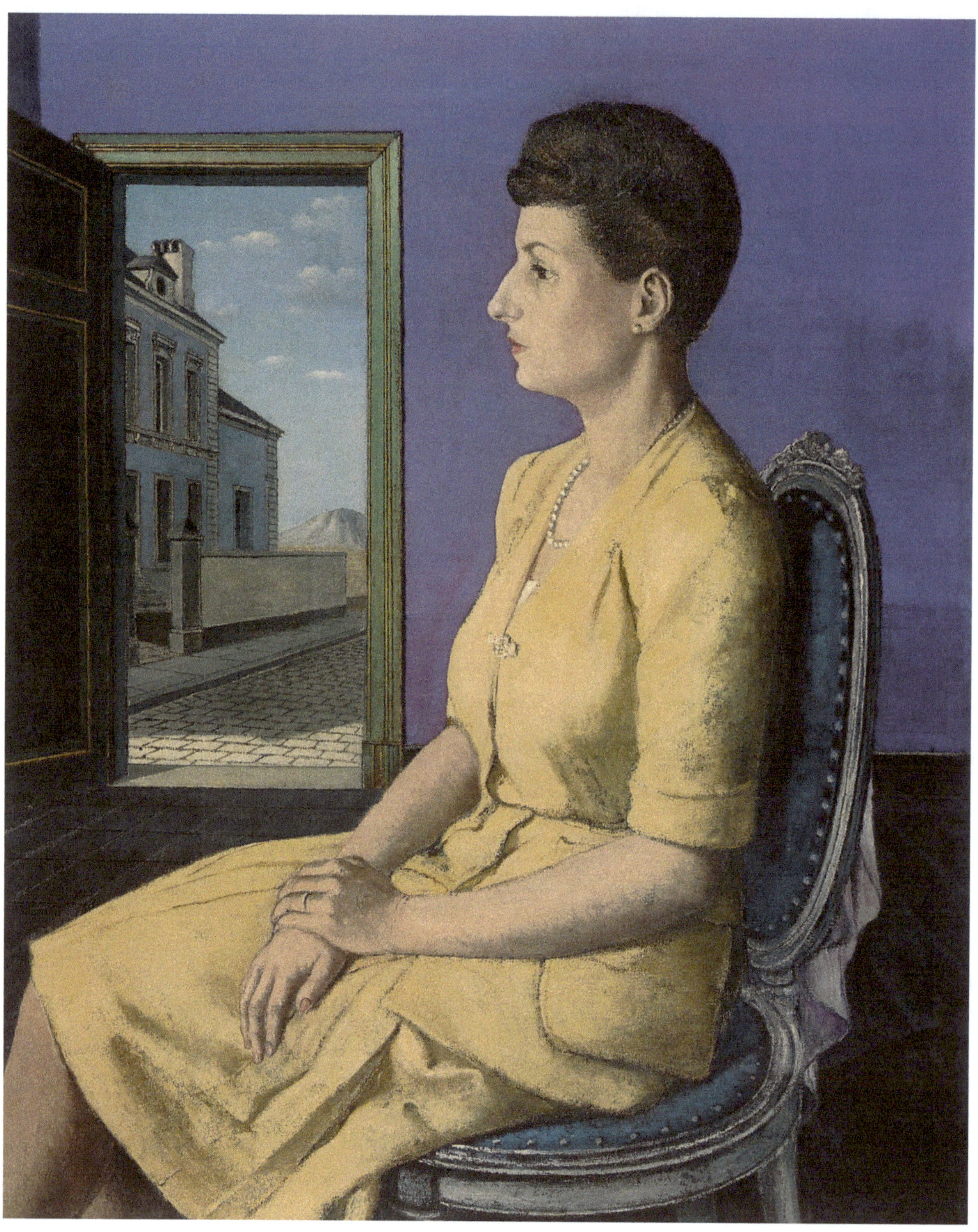

PAUL DELVAUX

(Antheit 1897- Veurne 1994)

Paul Delvaux was born in the Belgian town of Antheit. His father was a lawyer in Brussels. In 1916, he entered the Académie des Beaux-Arts, where he first studied architecture and then monumental painting. Delvaux was attracted, like all the Belgian Surrealists, to the work of James Ensor.

In 1922, at the age of twenty-five, Delvaux began to paint stations which became one of his lifelong themes and fixations. In 1930, at a fair in Brussels, he saw the Spitzner Museum. One of the pictures, a highly realistic painting, represented Doctor Charcot in front of a woman in a trance. The figures in this museum subsequently entered Delvaux's painting.

In 1934, at the Palais des Beaux-Arts in Brussels, the magazine *Minotaure* organised an exhibition of Surrealist works in which Delvaux encountered paintings by de Chirico, Dalí, and Magritte. By 1936, Paul Delvaux's pictures had already been exhibited alongside those of Magritte in Brussels, and in 1938, Delvaux took part in the international Surrealists' exhibition in Paris. In 1943, Delvaux painted a picture for Éluard called *The Echo*. Later, in 1948, they published

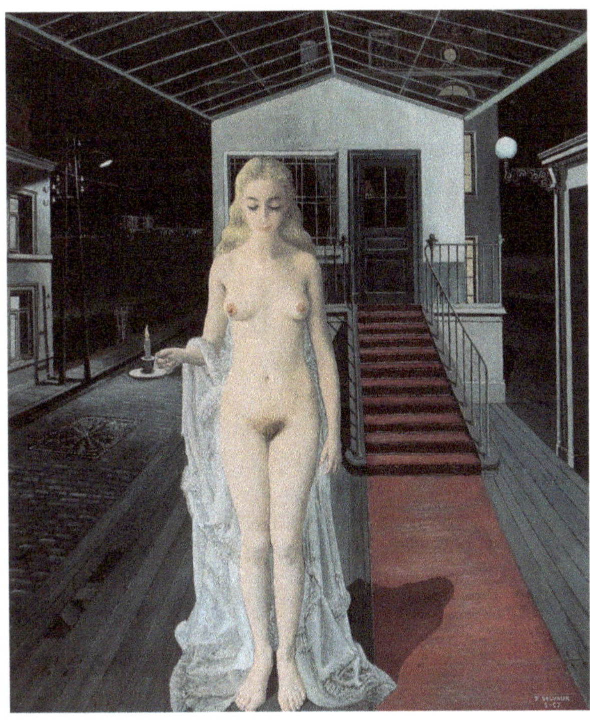

▲ **Paul Delvaux,**
Chrysis, 1967.
Oil on canvas, 160 x 140 cm.
Fondation Paul Delvaux, Saint-Idesbald.

◀ **Paul Delvaux,**
Madame Pollet, 1945.
Oil on canvas, 100 x 80 cm.
Fondation Paul Delvaux, Saint-Idesbald.

their *Poems, Paintings and Drawings* together in Geneva, and Éluard wrote his "Nights without Smile" in Delvaux's honour.

At the age of forty, Delvaux came to Surrealism much later than the other Surrealists. Delvaux absolutely rejected the notion that the subconscious, or the creation of pictures on the basis of dreams, was at all significant in his painting. Delvaux's first Surrealist pictures date from 1936, and the figures which later became constant presences had already made their appearance in them. *The Procession in Lace* depicts a procession of little girls dressed in white lace frocks. In another picture, *The Beauties of the Night*, half-naked girls appear once again in ancient architectural surroundings, and in the background, the hills of the Pays Noir of Wallonia can be seen. Sometimes he even reads the newspaper as he walks (*The Man in the Street*). He is reminiscent of the male figure in Magritte's paintings, in profile, in an overcoat and bowler hat.

Delvaux is ordinary and unremarkable. Even when something absolutely incredible is happening in the picture, he modestly slips past, and his silhouette vanishes into the distance (*Pygmalion*). Delvaux lived at a distance from the Surrealists's scandals, and in his painting a direct reaction to the current world events cannot be sensed. However, in the era of World War II, a mood of anxiety did appear in his paintings.

Sitting beside an unknown young woman, a skeleton imitates her pose and movement – life and death are always found together (*The Red Courtisans*; *The Woman and the Skeleton*). Skeletons take the place of living characters in biblical scenes.

The height of Delvaux's creative output occurred in the period between the 1940s and 1950s. During this period, all the figures he had created earlier continued to live in his pictures. They are gathered together, but each of them continues to live its own separate life, linked in no way to the others' lives. They exist in fantastic classical or renaissance towns in the quiet of a strange dream.

Another passion remains in Delvaux's painting. He always loved trams and trains. Trams appeared in his pictures in the 1940s. And in the 1950s, trains and stations become almost the only motif in his paintings. Day and night, the stations were empty but the trains always recede into the distance (*Little Station at Night*). Sometimes a nude figure appears on the station platform or in the waiting room. Venus sleeps on the sofa in the underpass below the railway line near Paul Delvaux's home at Watermael-Boitsfort (*The Blue Sofa*).

In the 1950s, Delvaux ranked alongside the most outstanding artists of Belgium and in 1977, Paul Delvaux was admitted to France's Academy of the Fine Arts as an associate foreign member. Paul Delvaux died in 1994 at the age of ninety-seven.

Paul Delvaux, ▶
The Entombment, 1957.
Oil on canvas, 130 x 120 cm.
Fondation Paul Delvaux, Saint-Idesbald.

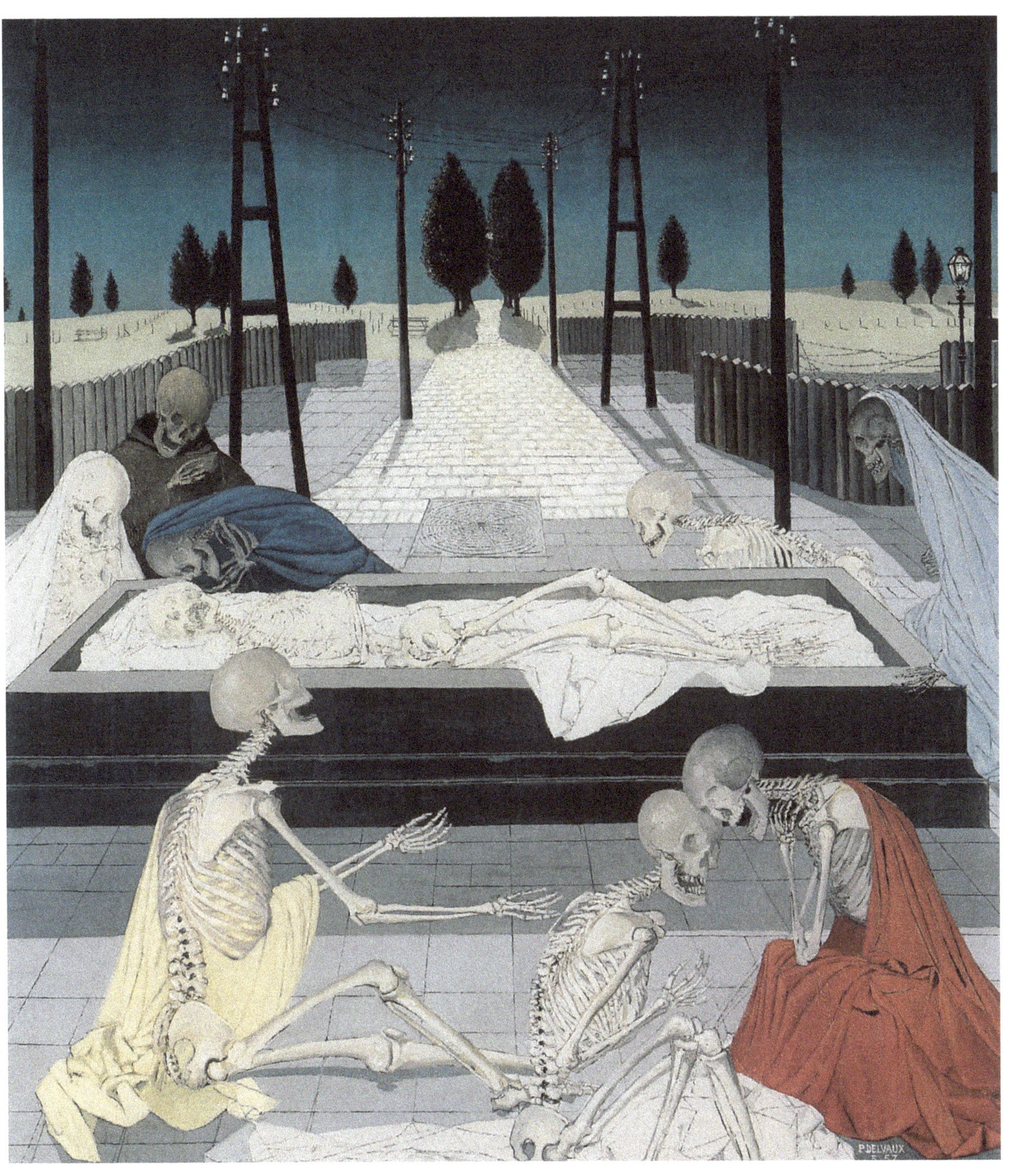

LIST OF ILLUSTRATIONS

ART HISTORY COLLECTION

Abstract Art

Art Deco

Art Nouveau

Baroque

Byzantine Art

Chinese Art

Cubism

Dada

Early Italian Art

Egypt Art

Expressionism

Gothic Art

Greek Art

Impressionism

Indian Art

Naive Art

Neoclassicism

Persian Art

Post-Impressionism

Realism

Renaissance

Pre-Raphaelites

Rococo

Roman Art

Romanesque Art

Romanticism

Surrealism

Symbolism

The Fauves

The Viennese Secession